DREAM *Big*
Step
SMALL

DREAM *Big*
Step SMALL

KRISTIN
OSTRANDER

Non-Fiction

Text copyright 2019 by Kristin Ostrander

Cover designed by Seedlings Online at www.seedlingsonline.com
Ebook production by E-books Done Right at www.ebooksdoneright.com
Typesetting by Atthis Arts at www.atthisarts.com

Every effort has been made to ensure that the content provided herein is accurate, up-to-date, and helpful to the reader at the time of this publishing. However, this is not intended to replace or treat any conditions, nor is it an exhaustive treatment of the subject. We encourage anyone to seek help with a professional counselor, therapist, or doctor where issues deem it necessary. No liability is assumed. The reader is considered responsible for your choices, actions, and results undertaken after reading this work.

Visit kristinostrander.com for more information about the author, updates, or new books.

ISBN 9781095707944

To Big O, LB, Bird, Sue-boo, and Mom.
There is not a heart big enough to hold the love I have for you!
Dream Big and take me with you.

~ xoxo

Author's Note

Just a little note for you.

I'm not sure why you decided to read this book.

Some of you may have stumbled upon it through a Facebook ad, or while searching for something new on Amazon. For others, you may have been listening to a podcast or my YouTube channel and heard me talk about my Amazon success.

No matter how you got to this book, I want to personally thank you.

By reading this book, YOU are now a part of my story. Even if you were already part of my life before this moment, you are now in the next chapter of my life. You have a piece of my heart and soul. A piece once tucked deep inside my heart. With many hours of sweat, tears, and deep soul searching, it has now entered your hands.

Within these pages is the story of a woman. She has many imperfections, and the raw and real truth of her struggle is revealed—the good, the bad, and the ugly. But she also has a story of hope. A story of triumph and of action.

A small story with big wins.

As my friend Christy Wright says, "You were created on purpose for a purpose."

Thanks for being part of mine.

INTRODUCTION

I know exactly where you are right now.

You're overwhelmed. Stuck.

You started a business, but now you're stressed about your never-ending to-do list. Maybe you want to switch directions, but starting something new is overwhelming. Perhaps you're thinking you have to choose between your business or being with your kids, and you're wondering if it's even possible to be great at both.

Friend, let me tell you—I have been there. Countless times. There is a better way. A different way.

A much more *simple* way.

In grabbing this book, you made a decision. You decided you wanted something different—whatever that is—and you wanted something bigger. That's what I'm going to help you figure out.

My life purpose is to help people through solving problems. I won't let you get away with just reading a book, so expect actions you *must* take even if they're scary. Or hard. Or intimidating. Expect vulnerable emotions. Expect battles you've been putting off for a while to resurface—only, for the last time.

This book was written to help you find, develop, and carry out your purpose one small step at a time. It will help you impact the world around you with your gifts, talents, and skills. My hope is that you'll finish this book with fire in your soul, so that fire will push you to take your next step, even if it's small.

I won't promise it will be easy. This is a journey of ups and downs. What I can promise is to remind you that you are not alone. To help you find your dream, and then see what it requires.

I'll guide you along a determined path that *will* take you to success. If you take the next step, big things happen.

Not overnight, but definitely over time.

Dream Big, Step Small is a blueprint. A map for you to follow if you have the courage to take one small step. That's all I'm asking. Just take this one step at a time—even if you have to read one page per day. That's a step.

That's progress.

Think of it this way—as long as you have breath in your lungs, you have a job to do. No matter what you're going through or have been through, God is not done with you until you close your eyes in death. That means we have dreams to build and purpose to find.

One step at a time.

Big Dreams are Possible

Confession time . . . I never dreamed big.

Believe it or not, I wasn't taught to dream big. I wasn't taught to dream at *all*, in fact. Go to school, get a job, pay bills—that's what I was taught. Do my best, and do the right thing. Let's be real . . . that's great. It's okay to learn that. In fact, I'm thankful for those life lessons because my world wouldn't be where it is today without them. But, most of us aren't conditioned to think bigger. We aren't even taught how.

Isn't that sad?

Here's the truth: if you want something different, better, and bigger, you have to learn how to conquer the struggles that are stopping you from getting there.

You *have* to.

But, it doesn't have to be stressful or overwhelming.

There is a different way.

When I had my second child, my husband and I had just moved into a townhouse that wasn't big enough for the four of us.

His job was feast or famine—money was tight. We were young and in debt. The constant struggle drove me to want something different.

I didn't like most of the options out there. *Was my only choice a four-year degree program with loads of student loans to pay and no guarantee of a job after graduation? Was climbing some corporate ladder the answer to our financial instability? Did I have to work nine to five? Did we have to live paycheck-to-paycheck with no back-up plan or savings? Would we rent a townhouse forever?*

Does it have to be this way?

I knew there had to be a way to do better. I wasn't even shooting for a lot—just a *little* better. There had to be a way to earn more income without sacrificing time with my family; I just didn't know how. In fact, I didn't even know what the job would be. But I knew what it *wouldn't* be. That's where I started.

It was *not* going to be working opposite shifts from my husband like two ships passing in the night. I was *not* going to have long days at home with kids and longer nights in college classes without a direction. I was *not* going to sit in a cubical repeating the same routine day in, day out. I was *not* going to sell make-up, skincare, or kitchen gadgets to my friends and family. While those things were a good fit for others around me, they weren't a good fit for me.

So, if I knew what it was *not* going to be, how did I figure out what it would be?

By taking the next small step.

The hope of creating a better life for yourself with big dreams is possible—my life is living proof. Bounced checks, bankruptcy, and foreclosure filled my life at one point. Now, with two businesses, one with $1.2 million in revenue and another that is fast approaching that mark, life looks much different.

Not perfect, but different. And definitely better.

Don't Dream Big . . . Yet

Dream Big is plastered all over the place.

Social media, hand-painted decorative signs at craft shows, on the covers of journals, a meme on Instagram. You name it; you can probably find this motto on it. In fact, even I just told you that dreaming big is possible.

But hold on.

The truth is that *not* dreaming big was the very thing that pulled us out of our financial mess and made me who I am today. Because here's the reality: the people who tell you to dream big leave out the best part. The roadmap to that dream.

While living paycheck-to-paycheck in our little townhouse, I loved the thought of a better life. All our needs would be met and maybe even the desirables too—like a newer car, music lessons, concerts, or a tropical vacation. (If you know me, I am: All. About. The. Beach.) That's all they were, though. Ideas. Thoughts. Fantasies.

Something for someone else, but surely not for us.

I'm an optimistic realist, which means I maintain hope that big dreams are possible but do not separate myself from reality. Let's face it: the struggle is real. Dreaming big just discouraged me. I'd think to myself, *We will never be able to afford a trip to Disneyland. We will never go to Hawaii. There is way too big of a gap from where we are to that far off place.*

I would write off dreaming big as *possible* but not *probable*.

Possible because I've heard many rags-to-riches stories. Not probable because our circumstances were unique.

It's too hard.

It's too overwhelming.

It will never happen for us.

All of those are very real—and very fair—thoughts. Dreaming

is scary, overwhelming, and challenging. So, what if we scaled back? What if I broke this up into smaller segments? Instead of looking at the overwhelming end game, what would happen if I focused on today? What would happen if we positively considered our biggest dream while looking at the very next move we could make to get closer to it?

That's what *Dream Big, Step Small* is all about.

THE POWER OF SMALL STEPS

I'm often asked what my secret is to running a six-figure and a seven-figure business *and* being a mom. How did I get over all the hurdles? My answer is always the same.

One step at a time.

This is more than just a saying—it's a life philosophy and strategy that can be applied to anything or anyone. I don't know about you, but when I see a seemingly insurmountable mountain, I want to run away. It's too big and too scary, and I don't feel equipped to handle it. I prefer not to tackle it.

The trouble is that oftentimes climbing the mountain is the only way to change things. You can run away for a time . . . but it will be waiting for you when you're done running.

Trust me.

Let's go back to my Disneyland dream that was, at the time, a seemingly insurmountable mountain. This time, let's apply the *Dream Big, Step Small* methodology. Instead of dreaming about the unattainable, expensive trip to Disneyland, let's research how much a budget hotel would cost. Could I earn a couple hundred dollars (as opposed to the thousands it seemed it would cost)?

Of course.

Applying this to your business—and your sense of overwhelm in it—is simple. Instead of focusing on making a million dollars, figure out how you'll make the next fifty.

Here's another example.

Tropical vacations are my thing. I've been on many of them now, but in the not-so-distant past, dreaming of a tropical vacation was something *other people* did. You know—rich people. (This was a money mindset issue I had that we will discuss later on.) Dreaming of a beach vacation seemed so far away from our cheap ramen noodle budget. But I still wanted it. Bad. So, I decided to step small.

Pocket change small.

I started taking small action steps like this:

1. Put all household change into a jar for a vacation fund. All loose change went into this jar daily.
2. Research budget-friendly places for a short anniversary trip.
3. Ask our friends if we could barter for their timeshare points to stay at their resort.
4. Booked vacations eight months in advance so we had enough time to save.
5. Earn an extra $50 per week for a vacation fund by selling five items on eBay each week.

At the time, I had more time than money, so I researched places that would have tropical weather, but would also be budget friendly.

Enter Miami in October.

The weather is beautiful, it's the tail end of hurricane season (which made it budget friendly), and our friends had timeshare points to sell to us. We booked in advance, which gave us plenty of time to save for airfare and spending money on our four-day trip. We didn't go to an all-inclusive resort on an island for a week. We started small. We did what we could when we could . . . all while dreaming bigger.

That was seven years ago. While writing this book, I did go to an all-inclusive resort on an island.

Stepping small over time gets you to big places.

STUMBLING BIG

Just like dreaming big can be overwhelming, stumbling big can be even scarier.

Yes, you will stumble.

That is why we step small. When we step small, we stumble small.

Dreaming big sometimes gives us the impression that we have to step big—and potentially, fail big. Fear often prevents us from dreaming because we stumble on thoughts like these:

- What if I fail?
- What if I never get to the big dream?
- What happens if I try, and it doesn't work out?
- What if I embarrass myself?
- What if someone is disappointed in me?

Friends, I am warning you now: You will fail a few times.

You will stumble.

You won't accomplish everything on the first try.

But, guess what? That's okay. In fact . . . it's normal. It's expected. That's why smaller steps are easier to take. If you fall, it won't hurt as much. Stumbling off a curb is less dangerous than plummeting from a tightrope, right? No matter what step you're taking, big or small, fear will still be there. (We'll deal with that in an upcoming chapter.)

Remember this: we are less afraid of small things.

Dream big. Really big. Mount Everest big. But then, step small. Prepare for the next little thing you can do. Prepare for balancing on the curb before moving to the tightrope.

Time is going to pass anyway. Would you rather sit at the bottom of Mount Everest and worry about falling, or focus on taking the next small step?

NOT ALL SUNSHINE AND RAINBOWS

I bet you think I'm gonna say that I stayed on a straight path to a million-dollar business and lived happily ever after. Right? Butlers, chauffeurs, and pool boys? Maybe you're thinking I went from $50 a week with my eBay business to a million-dollar Amazon empire in a year? In your dream, I probably hunkered down after that first small vacation, got focused, and started building a huge income within a month or two, right?

Uh, not even close.

It wasn't that easy, and it wasn't that pretty. Before we launch into the adventure of *Dream Big, Step Small*, I want to make one thing clear: this journey is not all sunshine and rainbows.

Eventually, I did build a seven-figure business. And, I do live a happy life. But, it took *years*. Fifteen-minute stretches of work. Sixteen-hour days. A whole lot of pivots and roadblocks along the way. I've been down the hard road. Many of them, in fact. My fridge has had nothing but crumbs, and my bank account nothing but cobwebs. I've been stuck in a job I hated while being separated from my kids. I lost my house. I dropped out of college.

I bet that sounds overwhelming and defeating.

It was, but I learned that it doesn't have to be.

Dream Big, Step Small will help you see your dream, and then make it happen. This book will show you that change is possible for you, too.

You can climb out of the hole you're in and back into the light even though it's not going to be all sunshine and rainbows. It's going to be hard. There will be times you will want to quit. It will be slower than you think. There will be times you'll feel hopeless. There may even be times where you'll have to start over.

Here is my promise to you.

There will be sunshine. Plenty of rainbows will find you each step of the way. I will show you how to take small steps to big dreams. I will encourage you and teach you. This isn't another rags-to-riches story. This is real.

This is gritty.

HAVE IT ALL

Unlike the rest of the world, I will tell you the truth. Here is your truth moment: This book is going to challenge you to think differently.

In our fast-paced, one-click-instant-reward society, we've been conditioned to strive for bigger, better, and faster. Everywhere you look, promises of quick riches, extremely fast weight loss, and picture-perfect extravagant lifestyles abound.

Let's challenge these illusions, and go against the grain to find the real truth.

The real truth is that you CAN have it all . . . but it doesn't come easy.

For all the extravagant lifestyles and tropical vacation pictures you see on social media, there is a story you don't see. The illusion of the *laptop lifestyle* where you can have a four-hour work week and everything is on autopilot is idolized, but rarely do you see the journey to that place.

What you don't see behind the scenes is the woman who worked fourteen-hour days for six months before someone noticed. She made personal sacrifices like less sleep, money, and time with friends to build a life she loves. Behind that tropical drink is her cutting costs and saving for that vacation for a year. You also didn't see her fail the first five times she tried before something finally worked.

With the advent of social media, we're becoming conditioned to think that everyone else has a picture-perfect life. Because we saw one viral video of someone who all of a sudden has it made, we think it's the rule—not the exception.

This is the truth: the person you see on that one video probably had 500 videos no one ever saw. For every landing someone sticks, there were hundreds of falls that left them bruised.

It is time to think differently from the social media portrayal that's shoving overnight success down our throats. Yes, you can have it all. But, you can't have it all without hard work. And, you can't have it all right now. Every success story has a much longer timeline than you've ever seen. Behind every successful woman is a long line (*years,* my friends, *years*) of conquered struggles, rivers of tears, and a boatload of the courage it took to get back up and try again.

Big dreams won't happen overnight, but they will happen if you take consistent steps toward the life you want.

You can have it all—but you'll have to do things differently in order to get there. I built my businesses looking at the very next thing I needed to do.

Dreaming big—but stepping small.

The Challenge

Dream Big, Step Small gives you the methods and strategies I've practiced on my way to reaching big dreams. Not only that, but I'm going to provide multiple *Step Small* action steps along the way. These will give you the small steps you need to make your big dreams happen. Look for those within each chapter. You'll find a list of more action items at the very back. To make life even easier, I'll summarize the Step Smalls from each chapter at the end, just so you don't have to thumb through every page when you come back.

If you're reading this, you believe this is possible for you too.

I believe it too.

The hardships, the roadblocks, and the insecurities you will face while building a business of your dreams are real. I've made poor investments that cost me thousands of dollars. I've lost money on unsellable products. I've created courses that didn't get sign-ups. I once made a poor hiring decision that compromised my business so much that I had to start over—with nearly nothing.

Friends, business is tough.

I've been there, and I'll guide you through these tough moments. We're going to go through mom guilt, time shortages, and overwhelm. We're going to do the ugly cry more than once. We're going to feel like we'll never make it, but I promise, you will. Because I've got secrets that will carry you to the other side of fear, and into a place where big dreams happen.

Are you ready for more?

Dream Big, Step Small is an adventure! We don't get there in a sprint. We don't need to have it all figured out today. We don't even need all the required skills just yet. (We'll learn those along the way.) We get there by taking one small step at a time. No overwhelm. Nothing bigger than one step.

Turning desire into small action steps means progress.

You ready for the challenge?

Chapter 1

THE STRUGGLE IS REAL

The first thing I'm going to do is let you know that the struggle is real.

I get it.

Owning a business is a struggle. Choosing your next big project is a struggle. Managing finances is a struggle. Being a mom is a struggle. My firstborn was very challenging. He was active from birth, always moving, wiggling, and getting into mischief. I always had to have one eye on him. Once, when he was three, while I was nursing my newborn, he unlocked the front door, ran into the parking lot, and climbed aboard the community rideshare bus. Running a business with him around?

The struggle is REAL.

How about when you have opened and closed three different direct sales businesses—hoping each time that this one would surely be the Midas touch. . . .

The struggle is REAL.

When your to-do list is longer than the paper it is written on, the laundry pile is taller than you, and everyone wants to know what is for dinner. . . .

The struggle is REAL.

When all you want is a hot shower, but that client emailed you again; you need to expand your business, but your budget has less wiggle room than your jeans; and, you need to hire help, but you are too paralyzed by fear to let go of control. . . .

The struggle is REAL!

Friends, I see you. I am with you. Even where I am today, I feel these things. Many people think that all these issues disappear when you reach a certain level. Nope! They stick around. But there are viable solutions and skills that make this journey easier and more fun. I had to learn many of them in hard ways.

In fact, I had to hit rock bottom before I could learn those lessons and get to where I am today.

It wasn't pretty.

THE BEGINNING OF THE END

We were determined to buy a house.

We paid off debts, saved for a down payment, and, as a working-class family, sacrificed many things to become homeowners. Our first house was a perfect fit for us! The best part? The pool. BBQs, hosting parties, the firepit . . . but mostly the pool.

This was our forever home.

When our third child was one week old, my husband Ben called home. "Kristin," he said, "I'm on my way to Urgent Care. I injured my shoulder at work." He was a commercial carpenter—we were no stranger to minor injuries. Unfortunately, I had no idea that *this* injury would change our lives forever.

My husband's injury required surgery. The healing process would lay him up for nearly six months. On top of that, we were denied workers compensation, which led to one of the lowest moments of my life. I had two young kids, a newborn, an injured husband, a very small online business, and forty-three dollars in the bank. No savings. No backup. And now, no source of income.

What were we going to do?

A huge weight to step up to the plate settled on my shoulders—but I didn't have any real work experience. Instant regret and feelings of utter failure set in. I hadn't finished college to help support my family or build savings. I should have finished like my dad said. Now I didn't have any marketable skills. Would my family starve? Shame on us for not having a backup plan!

These thoughts circled through my mind. I felt it was my fault.

Here I was, thirty years old, with nothing but a small online store and a year of waitressing experience. Rage, sadness, and disappointment in myself overwhelmed me—I felt as if I had let the entire world down. As a people-pleaser, this is the lowest of the low.

It would get worse.

Despite our war against our debt—filing for state assistance, food stamps, and government insurance—we couldn't get out of the hole. Negotiations with our mortgage company were fruitless. An attempt to short sale our home failed. I felt doomed to a life of just barely keeping the lights on.

Months after my husband's surgery and gradual return to work, we received the final notice that our home was being foreclosed. Our forever home was being stripped away. The place where we had been raising our children, having pool parties, and structuring the rest of our life. I am not gonna lie.

I freaked out.

THE BLESSING OF ROCK BOTTOM

Have you ever felt hopeless? Trapped in your circumstances? Felt like there was no way out? Me too.

Nothing can prepare you for that kind of pain.

After we lost our forever home—the one we were *supposed* to raise our children and play with our grandchildren in—we had no idea what to do next. Ben was back to working full-time. My online business was still small and struggling. That's a very lonely, lost place to be. The questions are relentless, and so is the guilt.

What now?

How do I start again?

Where do I start again?

On what path?

Is there another way?

The huge mountain of trouble we were facing seemed too big

and scary. With too many worries, doubts, and unknowns, I almost lost all hope. I needed to do something. Anything. I decided to step small. To be honest . . . that was all I could do.

Given my insecurities about the future, certain financial ruin, and crippling feelings of failure, I wasn't sure I had any hope left. We faced foreclosure, and there was no way around it. We couldn't go another way. We had to climb that mountain. So, I found one ounce of hope. That one ounce was enough to take one small step every single day. Pretty soon I was halfway up the mountain.

One small step at a time.

Hitting rock bottom was one of the biggest blessings in my life. Not only did it make me stronger and more resilient, but it also made me ask better questions. It forced me to find solutions. The good news is that when action is taken, no matter how small, despair gives way to hope. If you're at rock bottom right now: hold on. Better things will come when you step small. We recovered.

Just like you will.

THAT WAS THEN

Sometimes, I drive by the old "forever" house.

When I see it, I am instantly taken back to the last time I was inside. The walls were bare—with the exception of a few crayon marks behind where the couch used to be. My footsteps echoed in the empty halls. There were more stains on the carpet than I remembered. Emptiness and shadows filled every space. I walked alone from room to room, looking for what we'd forgotten. Nothing was left behind.

Except maybe my heart.

The mixed emotions get to me every time. So much despair, frustration, and grief.

And yet . . . now there's so much joy. When I mentally go back to that place, I quickly snap back to the present. My life today is so much better. I remember what I am doing right now. That's when the old feelings fade into my new reality. I grin as I drive away.

That was then . . . but this is now.

Chapter 2

DESIGN YOUR IAPW

Perhaps you've heard of the concept of the BHAG.

BHAG stands for *Big Hairy Audacious Goal,* an idea conceptualized in the book, *Built to Last: Successful Habits of Visionary Companies* by James Collins and Jerry Porras.

According to Collins and Porras, a BHAG is a long-term goal that changes the very nature of a business's existence. It has a clear-cut focal point and a finish line. It's what you're aiming at and working toward. It's bigger than you are comfortable with on purpose because it teaches you to aim higher even if you fall short.

I'll admit that I like the concept of a BHAG.

Although I didn't always believe in dreaming big, I am now 100% a believer in goals. They work if you set them properly. The problem is that I always felt defeated by the big, huge goal concept. It felt so far away, so unrealistic. Unobtainable. Thanks to managing my kids, my business, my house, and all the things, I always fell short when I tried to shoot *that* high. Aiming too high and constantly missing made me feel like a failure. I don't know about you, but I prefer to feel successful. That's why I had to change the BHAG concept up a bit to fit my circumstances.

Instead of a BHAG, I call it my IAPW.

Or my *In A Perfect World.*

The BHAG is very concrete, solid, and intimidating. A BHAG has a beginning and an end. It implies that there is ultimate success or failure. It's also intended to be outrageous and audacious on purpose, hence the name.

The IAPW concept is different.

It's more fluid and a bit more plausible. It's personal, flexible, and can change as your circumstances change. Now don't get me wrong, I know there is no such thing as perfect ... but *if* there were perfection, this would be your chance to craft it.

The IAPW scenario gives you a place to aim without the stress and pressure of meeting certain deadlines or falling short of something so gigantic. The IAPW is designed to reveal both the present and the future—but in bite-sized pieces. Instead of one BHAG, you can create several IAPW's that fit different parts of your life. Meals, homework, snow days, and daycare issues sure make a business BHAG difficult for working moms.

That's also how the IAPW is different. You can have different IAPW's for the shifting parts of your life. Why stick with one? Have several perfect scenarios!

The IAPW is even designed without the stress of having to think about this *big, huge thing*. You do it this way: Close your eyes and imagine what your perfect day would look like. Drift away with it for a bit if you need to. There's no stress or huge thinking or massive goals in this—just a happy, perfect day.

- Here's a little help to get you started:
- When will you wake up?
- What is the weather like?
- Who are you with?
- Where is your location?
- What are you wearing?
- What food would you eat?

As you begin to dream, ask more questions and add more layers. What would you spend time doing? How do you feel on this perfect day? There is nothing to hold you back here. This is your fantasy land. You can dream up whatever you want.

The practical side comes later.

My IAPW

To give you a better idea of what this would look like, here's my IAPW. (For my perfect day).

I wake up around 8 a.m. No alarm. I just wake naturally. The sun is shining, and it's beautiful outside. A warm breeze is blowing in off the water and into my beach house window. A steaming cup of hot coffee is in my hand while I sit outside, overlooking the water.

I have a time of prayer and devotions and finish my coffee. There is nothing immediately pressing that I must rush into, so I take a long walk on the beach. After that comes breakfast with my husband. I don't cook, and perhaps enjoy it from a local restaurant.

After breakfast, I get to work. Writing, helping people, doing a coaching call or recording a podcast, anything that makes me feel the most fulfilled and successful come first. After working for four or five hours, I return to my beach patio and read a chapter or two from a book. Learning new things or about new people thrills me.

Now I'm hanging out with my kids, hearing about their day, and just being with them. My energy is high—I'm not overwhelmed or overworked. I feel relaxed and ready to make something for dinner. I listen to a podcast while cutting up vegetables and preparing food. Our family sits together and eats while having a fun conversation.

After dinner, someone else does the dishes. I get to work on a project that delivers a result and a feeling of accomplishment. I am at peace and relaxed.

I wind down from the day with a glass of wine, a movie, or an episode of Island Living with my husband. Before bed is more reading and journal writing.

Bedtime is whenever I feel tired. I drift off to sleep without any stress over the next day.

This is my perfect day scenario.

The IAPW can be designed and applied to any circumstance—in life and in business. As you can see, my IAPW includes work. I love what I do! I can't imagine a perfect day without working in some capacity. But this is a broad IAPW encompassing a perfect day. Let's refine it a bit more and create a targeted IAPW for my work hours that day.

When I start to work, a short list of things to do awaits me.

The tasks on that list are things I love doing. Coaching calls. Writing. Recording podcasts. I feel relaxed, ready, and confident in taking care of these responsibilities.

While working, I learn something new and apply it to my business. I make a connection with someone. I have several people on my team, so we check in with one another. I am completely comfortable with my income and feel I lack nothing. I work four to five hours and feel accomplished when I finish. No pressure or stress hangs over me because I take on only what I can handle. I never need to say to my family that I need just one more minute.

There is enough time to do the things that are most important, which means I'm at peace with my tasks.

Feels good, doesn't it? Notice how the focus is on how I *feel*, not just what I'm doing. The IAPW is more about how you want to feel rather than meeting a goal. That's what makes the IAPW so powerful and so different.

And the beauty of an IAPW scenario is that it can change over time. It's fluid. You don't have to commit to one big thing (or stress about thinking of a big enough thing!) The IAPW can move with our busy, hectic, not-always-easy-to-run-a-business schedules. The IAPW still encourages you to dream big. (Living in a beach house? Yes, please! I love warm weather and sunshine and summer and water and sun.) The purpose is to visualize what your life would be like if you created it as a perfect fit.

The reality is, unless we hit the mega-millions lottery, we will have to work for a living. Fortunately, that doesn't mean you have to do something you hate or sacrifice everything good in life *now* to try to work for something better down the road. I'm here to tell you that you don't have to wait with a heavy heart, muttering under your breath, "Someday, we'll make that happen."

Someday is here.

You can take step smalls toward that perfect day right now.

Build several points of your IAPW into your life today. The IAPW design encourages you to start thinking about what you want to feel at the end of each day. You can do that right now!

It's time to get practical and close the gap between where you are today and your IAPW. As you read my IAPW, look closer at the picture I painted. There's an overarching theme of how I want to feel.

Peaceful.

At the end of the day, I don't want to feel rushed, pressured, or stressed out by dinner, children, and all the demands on my time. I want to feel accomplished, productive, and peaceful. That naturally means I could spend quality time with people I love, nurture myself physically and spiritually, and serve others in my business and my family. (Which just begets more peace!)

If we are honest with ourselves, we know there's a gap between our IAPW and our current situation. That's okay. In fact, that's normal. The beauty of stepping small is that there's something that can be done right now to narrow the gap between our present reality and our IAPW. Figuring out your IAPW is your next small step, but let's break this down into even easier steps.

DESIGN YOUR IAPW

Design Your IAPW Step One: You can design one overarching IAPW or several different ones. I prefer to create personal, business, and financial IAPWs. Here's some help to get you started on different IAPW's that might help you be more successful in your business:

Financial:

- What does your bank account look like?
- How do you feel when you look at the numbers?
- What do you plan to do with the money?
- How does your partner or family feel about the money?
- Do you have an accountant that gives you good advice?
- Are all your books up to date?

Emails:

- What does your inbox look like?
- How do you feel about it?
- How long will you spend managing it?
- Will you outsource it to someone else?
- Who are the emails from?
- Do they bring positive feedback?

Self-Care:

- What do you do?
- Do you do it by yourself or with someone?
- Do you get a massage?
- A haircut?
- A pedicure?
- How do you feel at the end of it?
- How many hours are focused on self-care?

Now it's time to sit back, relax, and imagine your perfect scenario. Write it in a journal, type it out on your computer, or use the power of your imagination to really visualize it in your head.

See how easy that is? If you're feeling brave, come share it in the *Dream Big, Step Small* Facebook community[1].

Step Small 1: Let's design the IAPW scenario for your business. What is all you ever wanted? What is the ultimate feeling you desire at the end of your workday?

1. Decide how you want to feel at the end of the day today. Narrow it down to one word.
2. Write down three tasks that will get you there.
3. Do one of those tasks.

Example: I want to feel *peaceful*. When I am presented with an opportunity, event, or a work project, I must run it through the filter of *peace*. If this opportunity will throw my life off balance and become a peace disruptor, I will respectfully decline. No one will die. They will not hate me for saying "no." I will be better off for protecting my *peace* than if I accept a fun but stressful project.

Design Your IAPW Step Two: Chart the next step to get you closer to your business IAPW.

This is where we examine how you want to feel. Remember how my IAPW was centered around peace? Let's find your feeling. Your word.

In fact, finding your word is our main action step here. Because let's face it: choices are ultimately emotional. Your next action step toward your IAPW should always be something you can control.

Every choice in your life comes down to how you want to *feel*.

---

1 Join our Facebook group here: https://www.facebook.com/groups/dreambigstepsmall/

We make choices based on what we think is best for us in that moment, even if those choices are negative. If we choose french fries over salad (and we definitely know they aren't good for us), in that moment, we *feel* fries will be more satisfying than salad. We believe we'll *feel* more satisfied with fries, therefore justifying the poor choice in the name of comfort and ease.

Now we examine the tasks, people, and events that bring the most stress. Reduce or eliminate those, whether they're outside pressures, internal, or self-imposed. Let's be real. A LOT of our stress points are self-imposed.

Here's one of mine.

Like many working women, I allow myself to say *yes* to too many things. One day, my daughter's teacher was looking for someone to volunteer once a week to practice literacy exercises with the kids. During the meeting, all the other parents were signing up to volunteer. I felt obligated to sign up too.

I have freedom and flexibility in my work-from-home schedule to do things like this, I told myself as I stared at the clipboard coming around. *So, I should do it, right?*

To be honest, I don't love being in the classroom. Baking homemade treats or sending supplies is a much better fit for how I prefer to contribute.

Cue the mommy guilt.

When the sign-up sheet came around to me, the only thing left was a year-long, two-hour weekly commitment. Out of guilt . . . I signed up. I'll admit, this happens to me a lot. I'm a people-pleaser. I want to make everyone happy, even if it makes me unhappy!

I should have known better.

Instant regret set in. My schedule certainly has flexibility, but was I obligated to spend it this way? Still, I committed, so I showed up. After several months of showing up to this "I need to prove I am a good mom who cares about her kids' education" duty, I was completely stressed. Stressing over the commitment caused me to fall behind on other more important things. The thoughts in my head weren't kind.

I did this to myself. Again. What was I thinking? Why did I do that?

Here's the truth: there's always an opportunity to make a new choice.

Right then, I had the choice to live stressed out, or withdraw my commitment in the name of peace of mind. For some of you, the thought of backing out of a commitment would be worse than being stressed out and overbooked. I hear you. My people-pleaser cringes at the thought of disappointing anyone.

But I had to be honest with myself: I'd made a bad decision, and I would have to live with the consequences no matter what path I chose.

In this case, I decided to base my decision on wanting peace, because that was in alignment with my IAPW. The temporary sting of other people's judgment was part of the price I'd pay. The ultimate result allowed a return to a more peaceful balance. The added bonus? Learning to make choices based on what aligned me with my IAPW instead of my guilt.

Now, back to you: it's time for you to decide how *you* want to feel? Productive? Peaceful? Energetic? Present?

Let's look at a financial example.

If your IAPW's focus is to *eliminate debt* or *save for retirement*, the emotion tied to that is security. You want to feel secure—with enough money for a comfortable retirement. Your next step could be making a plan to put money from each paycheck into a retirement account. That helps close the gap between your current insecurities. Even if it is only $25, you'll have more comfort (or peace!) in the moment.

Sounds a lot less overwhelming than trying to save a million dollars for retirement by age sixty-five, doesn't it? If you start saving at thirty years old, that would require $550 per week for thirty-five years.

Oh my! Too big!

Step small, friends, and you can still dream big.

Step Small 2: What is one thing in your life right now that doesn't align with your IAPW scenario? Take one step to remove it.

Step Small 3: What is one thing you can do to reduce or eliminate stress points in your life? Write your list and keep it where you can see it, or better yet, take action right now.

START NOW

A few final thoughts on IAPW's.

We should never complain about what we allow in our life.

We make choices that give permission for circumstances or conditions to exist in our day-to-day routine. If someone mistreats us, and we don't set boundaries, we're giving them permission. If we put more on our plate than we can handle, we are responsible for the overload. No IAPW will actually work if we constantly get in our own way!

Instead, I challenge you to troubleshoot your life by building your IAPW in a way that prevents those things, people, or circumstances from derailing it. When you clearly define what you want (and how you want to feel), it becomes easier to make choices that align with your goals.

By the way, this holds true in all areas of life, especially business.

How great of a CEO (yes, you are CEO, more on this later) can you be if you're a stressed out, overbooked mess? Let's change that right now. Armed with the knowledge in this book, you *can* follow the blueprint to your IAPW.

Don't look at the far future yet. Look at the very next thing you can do. If you look for the small step every day, over time, you'll have everything you ever wanted. I've found that the secret to getting everything you want is hoping for it, planning for it, taking the next small step toward it, and being grateful for each moment. The sky's the limit when you commit to your IAPW.

Now it's your turn.

Step Smalls in this Chapter:

1. Design the IAPW for your business.
2. What is one thing in your life right now that doesn't align with your IAPW scenario? Take one step to remove it.
3. What is one thing you can do to reduce or eliminate one stress point in your life?

Chapter 3

SELF-DISCOVERY

Thanks to your new IAPW, we're going to start this chapter out a little different. In fact, we're going to figure out your dream job.

If you think you already have your dream job, go through this process anyway. You may learn new things about yourself you never acknowledged that will better equip you on your path.

Your dream job enables you to make the best possible contribution to your family and the world. I believe each one of us is gifted by God with a unique set of skills, gifts, and talents. How we use our gifts may change over time as we move through seasons of our life, but what will never change is our responsibility. We need to contribute these unique gifts to the world.

If you have a passion for something, it's there for a reason. Whether that's teaching thousands of people on a stage or making soup for a homeless shelter, you were created to make an impact on the world around you.

It's high time you stepped into that role.

Everyone has a different story. You have life experiences, skill sets, relationships, and talents that are unique to you. We all have skills we don't realize are valuable because they come naturally to us. It's just who we are. I am going to help you tap into those valuable resources you have been hiding by helping you find your calling—your dream job.

MINE FOR GOLD

A quick caveat here: this isn't just for people who don't have a job already. Are you working at a job, but it's not your dream? Are you working your dream job now? Dreams shift and change—so do careers. Read this regardless of where you are in your career. You never know when you might need it.

For this Step Small, you have to get real with yourself.

Self-discovery is a very important part of stepping into your purpose. I call it mining for gold because we're finding the shiny, beautiful parts already within you. Mining is not all sunshine and rainbows. It is dirty, dangerous, difficult work. If you've ever seen the TV Show *Gold Rush,* you know what I mean. All day and night they toil in the half-frozen mud, digging deep to find the rich pay-dirt that will yield millions. Their machines break down. They become irritable. Some quit before they ever find gold. While profitable, the work is difficult, dirty, and scary.

Prepare yourself, friend.

Together, we are going to mine for *your* gold—to find your dream job by going through the questions below. This is a bigger small step. If your time is limited, which I know it probably is, answer a few questions at a time until the list is complete. More on how to get things done in smaller faster steps in Chapter Six.

Step Small 1: Answer the questions below.
If you struggle with answering these questions about yourself, ask someone you trust for an honest opinion.

Self-Discovery Questions

   a.   What's your cultural background?
   b.   Where did you grow up?
   c.   What religious influences did you have?
   d.   What type of jobs have you had?
   e.   What type of education do you have?
   f.   What sports or extracurricular activities have you participated in?
   g.   What subject did you love in high school or college?

h.   What are your hobbies?

i.   What are you passionate about? *(i.e., what sets your soul on fire and gets you excited?)*

j.   What do you always talk about? (Problem or passion)

k.   What do you spend most of your free time doing?

l.   What are you good at? What areas do you have talent?

m. What types of things come easy and natural to you?

n.   What gives you energy?

o.   If you had an extra hour in your day, what would you do with it?

p.   Finish this sentence, "If I could do any job in the world, I would . . ."

q.   What would you do for free just because you love doing it?

r.   What would be the coolest thing to get paid to do? *Get crazy here. Be ridiculous.*

Now take this list, and let's start mining—narrowing your options for your dream job.

To narrow your options, pick the top three things from this list you are knowledgeable about, skilled at, and passionate about. Which one of these things makes you the most excited? If you're good at organization but don't enjoy it, don't build a business around that. Do you like designing, but not for other people? Pass on that idea.

You can learn and develop new skills, but what you can't duplicate is *passion*. Go with your heart and not *what will make the most money* strategy.

Once you've finished mining for the golden nuggets of passion that interest you, move onto the next Step Small.

Step Small 2: Narrow your list of possible dream job options to three.

In all businesses, there will be things you don't like doing. Not many people are passionate about taking out the trash, but those things still need to be done. Keep your main passion in mind while understanding you will never love 100% of the tasks in any business. Eventually, you can outsource tasks you don't enjoy. What you can't outsource is passion, talent, and your unique, personal perspective.

This is when we get to dream a little bigger.

We want a business, not a hobby. Businesses make money. What are the current opportunities available for you to use your God-given abilities in earning a living?

Here is a sampling of the ways you can create income with your passion:

Create digital products (courses, classes, books, videos, podcasts).

Create physical products (books, journals, art, crafts, handmade items, furniture).

Offer a service (coaching, consultations, evaluations, teaching, training, catering).

Open a store, office, or physical location.

Become an independent contractor in your desired field.

Find a traditional job that fits your criteria.

Become a speaker.

Step Small 3: Pick one option from your dream job list and research ways other people are making money in that field.

The best feeling in the world is to get paid to do something you love. Chase passion, and money will come. Get serious about the impact, not the income, and you'll be amazed at the things you will accomplish one small step at a time.

Business Identity Crisis

Unfortunately, you won't wake up one day and arrive at your dream job.

It takes a lot of pivoting and discipline to figure it out. I've taken many twists, turns, and detours to get where I am today. I have no doubt that there will be plenty more to come! Here is one of the biggest twists I experienced—my business identity crisis.

I remember this like it was yesterday.

Finally, the day both of my children would go to school came. Don't get me wrong: I love my kids. I also love a calm, quiet house, which is very hard to come by with small children. Having several hours to myself felt like a treasured gift. Do you ever feel like you are never alone? Especially in your own home? Sure, I could go to Starbucks while my husband held down the fort, but home alone for a few hours a day, *every* day, to work on my business sounded like bliss.

Except . . . freedom wasn't what I'd expected.

The transition from full-time diaper changing, potty training, constantly-trying-to-prevent-the-house-from-being-destroyed-by-two-little-people mode, to five quiet mornings to myself was a bit rocky. I expected to make a plan to utilize my time and get to work doing what I'd always done: work on my eBay business.

Instead, I found myself unsettled and distracted.

My mind began to wonder about other career options. Eight years of being a stay-at-home-mom with an eBay store had passed, but I hadn't given much thought to what I would do when I finally had more time.

So, I did. I gave it some thought.

This is one of the first times I can recall writing down a few dream job ideas. *What would I consider a fun job?* I asked myself. After all—this was my new reality.

My list was called, *Things I'd Love to Get Paid For*. Some of the ideas were worth exploring, and some were never going to be a reality. I love to sing, but let's be real, I wasn't going to audition for *American Idol*. So, I moved on to the next thing on the list.

Cake Decorating.

I Give You Permission to Try . . . and Fail

Anyone remember *Ace of Cakes* on the Food Network? How about *Cake Wars* or *Cake Boss*?

Making cakes as beautiful as those was my new idea. I had messed around with cakes for years, but created nothing Pinterest-worthy. I loved to decorate cakes and had a knack for it, but I needed training. After my self-discovery questions, I took the idea of becoming a professional cake decorator to my husband. Being the supportive husband he is, he indulged my idea but asked, "What about your eBay store?"

I laid out a plan to keep up with my store and take a professional cake decorating classes on the side. Excitement filled me. This was something I loved to do, and I was ready for something different and new.

Much to my dismay, I couldn't jump straight into cake decorating class. I had to take beginners classes like *Food Safety* and *Culinary 101*. I learned fancy new words and professional chopping skills . . . but what I really wanted to do was make cakes. Eight weeks later, my beginning cake decorating class began. Sheer fun—I loved it. I bought all the required tools, books, and accessories, and then learned how to use them. I acquired new skills and new recipes to make cake and icing the way the pros do it. It was *awesome*.

Then, reality set in.

Before I finished my first class, I received my first for-profit cake order. A friend asked if I'd make a birthday cake for her son in the form of a book cover of his favorite book, *The Hunger Games*. Not too difficult—the cake would be mostly black with words and the famous Mockingjay logo. I took the job . . . but immediately panicked.

Perfection, precision, and correctness had to happen. It had to taste and look like a professional cake because she was paying me. If I was going to collect money, it had to be the best work I had ever done.

The design stressed me out. My piping skills were not the greatest yet, and black icing is *hard* to make. (Plus, fondant tastes gross, right?). Would I be able to remember what I'd been taught? Would they like it?

I spent fourteen hours on that cake, freaking out the whole time.

At one point, I scraped the entire top off and started over with only three hours to redo it. Then, I stressed even more about the time crunch I'd just put myself in by starting over. I cried, I cussed, and I was on my feet for fourteen hours.

I was in way over my head.

After crying on my husband's shoulder, he whispered to me, "Is this stress worth it?" No, it wasn't. I had started cake decorating as a labor of love for my own children, but the moment I tried to turn it into a business, all the joy drained out. Intense stress set in.

I finished the cake (which was a hit!), but it was my first and last for-profit cake. After that day, I vowed to never make a cake for money ever again. For love? For my kids? As a gift or a request for a loved one? Sure. For money?—not for any amount.

The truth was, I discovered something important.

I loved cake decorating, but not for money. This was not going to be my dream job, but that was okay. It was necessary to give it a really good effort to come to this conclusion.

Finding your dream job isn't fast or easy. It takes trial and error.

Try a few things on your list—but don't quit too soon. Cake decorating had my full attention for six months. I didn't try it for a few weeks and quit when it was hard. Jumping from one thing to the next when things get difficult isn't going to work.

That's why starting with something you love is such a priority. If you love it; it has potential. But just like cake decorating, loving something isn't enough. You've got to pursue it and try it.

I finished my cake decorating class for that semester and canceled the rest. Since then, I've made cakes for friends and family, but have happily left professional cake decorating to other people.

What Not to Do

Sometimes knowing what you *don't* want will help you discover what you *do* want. Many women try numerous things before they arrive at their dream job. This is perfectly acceptable.

Listen up friends—if you've tried every home-based business opportunity, changed your college major several times, crafted, waitressed, hosted parties for nail wraps or essential oils or Tupperware, or sold vacuums door-to-door, I am here to congratulate you.

This does not mean you are a quitter or a failure or that somehow you, yet again, couldn't make something stick.

It means you are a freakin' rockstar.

This means you were brave enough to try something new. It means you were strong enough to make a change when things weren't working out. It proves you aren't willing to settle for something less than your IAPW. I applaud you. This shows you're willing to try. You probably haven't found your dream job yet, but you have a resume of what it will never be. That is progress, my friend.

You are halfway there.

Before you pop the bubbly and celebrate your bravery, I'm gonna get real with you: There is a flip side to this.

You need to examine the reasons why things didn't work out.

Sometimes you're enamored by the sunshine and rainbows someone is promising if you invest in a certain business. Other times, you may have chased the lofty idea of quick-and-easy riches. Perhaps a new adventure sounded like a blast, and you couldn't help yourself. Whatever got you in, something also got you out.

Step Small 4: Write down two business opportunities you've started and stopped. Why didn't they work? If you haven't started and stopped any businesses, list a time in your life when you tried something new, and it didn't work out (sport, musical instrument, hobby). Why didn't it work?

But there's something else to this.

When you're pursuing your dream job, there are a few things I don't want you to do. As you go through this process, there will be ups and downs and changes. That's normal. But women are often very critical of themselves.

Stop it.

You'll sabotage your own success if you focus on what you aren't. Here are some things you may *not* do as you step into self-discovery:

1. **Don't beat yourself up.** You tried a few things, you gave it great effort, and it didn't work out. Remember the Amazon Fire Phone? Probably not, because Amazon released it and pulled it after a year because it was a total flop. It happens to the best of the best. They didn't beat themselves up or close up shop. They moved on to pursue another new idea. So can you.

2. **Don't call yourself a failure.** Failing only occurs when you stop putting in effort. If, in the past, you decided to take a different path, you didn't stop putting in effort. You just

put that effort somewhere else. Getting it wrong means you learn and try again with a new perspective and more experience. It's all data—not failure. Consider your mistakes as experiments, which are procedures used to discover something. You discovered what didn't work. Now that you've gotten that out of the way, you're free to experiment in a new way.

3. **Don't expect perfection.** If you set your sites on perfection, you'll live in a constant state of disappointment. Remind yourself that you're a beginner, and it's ok to make mistakes. Mistakes are as common as breathing, and they won't kill you. Use them as fuel to improve.

BUT DID YOU DIE THOUGH?

This may sound a bit funny (or even harsh to some of you), but my teenage daughter and I say this to each other all the time. For any of you who have a teenage girl in your life—the struggle is REAL! The sass, drama, and sarcasm rival that of a *Real Housewives* diva any day of the week.

Every day when she comes home from school, she likes to unleash all the craziness of her day. She sits next to me in my office and unloads all the drama, how much she hates school (aka prison) and especially people. Unlike her social, never-met-a-stranger-talk-to-anyone mom, my daughter is *not* a people-person.

One day, she had one complaint after another—most of them petty. Slightly annoyed, I turned to her and said, "But did you die though?" We both laughed. She said, "No. But it sorta felt like that."

I completely understood what she meant.

When our house foreclosed and everything was falling apart, there were times I thought I was dead inside. Hopeless. Stuck. Constantly fearing the worst. No matter how I felt, as long as I wasn't dead that meant God wasn't done with me yet. I could get up and start over. I could take a step in a different direction, make a new choice. We didn't die, so we had a chance to take another step.

But did you die though? is a small, simple, (and a tad bit sassy) reminder that we face hardships . . . but we will survive. Bad stuff happens. We have horrible days, but we won't die from them. If you survived, it means you still have time for a better day, a reset, an apology, a new start, and a different perspective.

Step Small 5: Name a time in business where you failed. Write what happened in the aftermath of this failure. HINT: you didn't die—so what really happened? How did you recover?

STEP SMALLS IN THIS CHAPTER:

1. Answer the provided self-discovery questions within the chapter.
2. Narrow your list of possible dream job options to three.
3. Pick one option from your dream job list, and research ways other people are making money in that field.
4. Note two business opportunities you've started and stopped and why they didn't work for you.
5. Name a time in business where you failed. Write what happened in the aftermath of this failure. HINT: you didn't die—so what really happened? How did you recover?

Chapter 4

TRUST THE FACTS, NOT THE FEELINGS

So, you've designed your IAPW, and you've narrowed your dream job options. Now, let's talk about another problem that tends to crop up just when you're inching closer to greatness.

Fear.

It's one of the biggest struggles in business and in life.

I could probably write an entire book on fear. The way it limits the enjoyment of new things, holds us back from bigger and better adventures, and prevents growth. As business grows, so do opportunities. So does fear.

This chapter is strategically placed here—you need to know how to conquer this problem before we press harder into your IAPW.

WHAT IS FEAR?

When I began teaching online, I loved it. I dreamed of being on a stage, sharing my knowledge and inspiring everyone. There was just one problem: fear left me paralyzed.

I knew what I wanted, but I was a complete rookie. I had never spoken on a stage before. (although, I had given hundreds of talks through my online show, podcast, and other interviews.) Speaking live wasn't a problem—but I did that alone in my office behind a camera. That's quite different than a room full of eyeballs staring back at you.

I kept feeling the push of my dreams and the pull of my fears. The painful battle waged for a long time—from one side to the next. My IAPW would lead me on a search for speaking opportunities . . . then, my fear would tell me I wasn't ready. Back and forth. I found no peace!

One day when I was listening to a podcast, I felt very connected to the lady being interviewed. My expertise fit well with her audience and connecting to her organization would be a good fit for my business. She had an event coming up and was accepting applications for speakers. The fire in my soul flared. I rushed to the website. *This,* I thought, *is surely my dream opportunity.*

It could have been.

I began reading the application and even started to fill it out. Then, a question that filled me with fear popped up.

List other events where you have spoken and links if you have them.

Fear rushed in. My courage deflated. I leaned back in the chair. Tears welled up in my eyes as I slammed my laptop closed. (Sometimes fear is subtle—but this time it wasn't.)

"You've never spoken anywhere else," whispered the voice in my head. "They won't accept you."

"You are going to screw it up anyway; just forget it."

"You are not good enough."

"You don't know what you are doing."

"No one will give you a chance."

These words filled my head, and I believed them. I opened my laptop and deleted the application. That could have been an amazing opportunity to do something new. Instead, I let fear steal it away.

Fear is a feeling. It's *real.* Even though it's often irrational, it's an actual emotion that's quite intense. Our bodies physically react with racing heartbeats, adrenaline rushes, sweating, and even fainting. Fear is our body's natural fight or flight response to danger. Most fears are thoughts created by our imagination to make reality seem scarier than it is.

So, let's talk about spiders.

I'm afraid of spiders. I hate spiders. When I see a big one, I scream, run, and get someone to come and kill it. If I get close to it, I'm convinced it will jump on me, bite me, and I will die. Anyone ever see the movie *Arachnophobia*? I saw it when I was ten, and it scarred me for life. Those people died!

Even though it's a bit irrational, this is how I *feel* about spiders.

Just like I feel about spiders, we're afraid of failing. We fear success. We fear being alone or getting sick. We fear being embarrassed or judged. We fear displeasing people. We fear the unknown. We fear death. Or, even worse, spiders. (Yes, spiders are worse than death. Don't judge me.) When we hesitate to try something new or make progress, we're acting out of fear.

Sugarcoat it any way you'd like. Call it worry, concern, anxiety, whatever you want. It's all fear. So, let's clearly define fear so we can understand it. Once we understand something, we can learn to take control of it—and not let it get in the way of our new IAPW and dream job.

"The cave you fear to enter holds the treasure you seek."—Joseph Campbell

Why Do We Have Fear?

Fear is best defined *as an unpleasant emotion caused by believing that someone or something is dangerous, threatening, or likely to cause pain.*

No wonder we want to avoid such things!

Although there are many debates on whether fear is natural or learned, the general consensus is that it's both. We naturally fear certain things—it's our body perceiving imminent danger and sending a warning signal to our brain. That creates a defense mechanism in our brain that attaches to that moment to protect us from the perceived threat.

As we build up negative experiences and feelings, we protect ourselves by avoiding things we feel threatened by. Our fear comes from *assuming* the future is based on the past. This stems from revisiting old experiences like failures, uncontrollable circumstances, tragedy, pain, and other unanticipated events that left us with painful feelings. Fear causes us to avoid certain situations because we assume the same result from the past will reoccur in the future.

My *fear* of spiders is based on an assumption from my past. I watched scary movies with spiders, and I assume all spiders are going to kill me. Anyone been poked by a needle and feel terrified of them now?

We try to protect ourselves by using avoidance. We base our decisions on previous experiences and the negative feelings that came with them. No one wants pain. No one wants hardship. We do things to avoid what we *think* will cause harm or pain.

Business is no different. We face a constant flow of choices as business owners. If we make choices based on fear ... we won't be in business long. If we're constantly putting off things that are difficult or scary, we won't progress. The root of procrastination really is fear.

The good news?

Learning to overcome fear is a skill anyone can learn.

Turn fear into fuel. Harness it to grow your business. If you want something you've never had, then you've got to do something you've never done. We all have fear. We can choose to let it control us, or we can learn to work through it. I know it isn't easy, but anything worth having will take work. You *can* learn new skills.

Remember—we're stepping small. There are a few strategies over the years that have helped me move past the fear of what I *feel* about a situation and embrace what is true, the *facts*.

Step Small 1: Take sixty seconds and write down as many of your fears as you can think of. Remember that no one is looking or judging. Be real with yourself.

Glenn Sparks, a communications professor at Purdue University who specializes in the cognitive and emotional impact of the media, said, "Studies show we can overcome some of our fears by continued exposure to them. By constantly exposing ourselves to our fears, our tolerance for them will grow."

By taking action, despite how we feel, we start to understand that we weren't in as much danger as we thought. We did the hard thing, and we didn't die! We survived. The scary thing isn't as bad as our imagination dreamed, which means we have a bit more confidence to try it again.

SMALL START, BIG FINISH

"If you are faithful in little things, you will be faithful in large ones."
—Luke 16:10a

We never know where life will take us.

I would have laughed if someone had told me fifteen years ago that I'd be creating video courses with a woman who lives a thousand miles away from me, while writing a book, and traveling around the country teaching people to make income online. I didn't start that way. I started with a willingness to try something new.

I started small.

So small, in fact, that falling into my dream was almost an accident.

Selling on Amazon has been a very profitable business for me. I first shared my experience with Amazon success on a live-streaming webcast hosted by Scanner Society (formerly Scanner Monkey) in 2014.

Cordelia Blake (the co-founder and host of the show) invited me on for an interview after seeing my comments in their Facebook community. I loved sharing my experience with e-commerce, as well as giving tips to new sellers. I wanted to help people, so I answered questions about selling on Amazon whenever I could. This was a live-streaming, weekly video program geared toward people wanting to start and grow Amazon businesses. My excitement for the show nearly overcame me. When I was there with Cordelia, I felt something I'd never felt before.

A *pinch me* moment.

That's the kind of moment when you have to pinch yourself to make sure you aren't dreaming. A moment so true and right that nothing can ruin it. Those are the moments when you feel the fire in your soul that gives you energy, ideas, and goosebumps. A *pinch me* moment says to you, *I was meant to do this.*

Being with live viewers and sharing my knowledge thrilled me. I felt at home, comfortable, and inspired. I wanted to do more. My heart seemed to be made for it.

One viewer made a comment that they'd love for me to have my own show so I could share more. That comment stopped me in my tracks. I thought about it a lot. I wasn't a huge Amazon seller at the time, but I had definitely overcome a lot of hurdles.

The doubts set in. Negative self-talk tried to kill the idea.

> *I don't have enough to share.*
> *I am not a big enough seller to share anything of value.*
> *No one would listen.*
> *There aren't many women teaching about Amazon.*

But that *pinch-me* moment was too strong. I loved answering questions. I wanted to tell everyone everything I knew. Asking, "Why *not* me?" silenced those doubtful voices. What did I have to lose? What if I never have that *pinch me* moment again? *Why not me* was enough of a catalyst to get me thinking about it.

That's a small step, by the way.

A few weeks after the show one of the viewers reached out to me via Facebook. His name was Rob Watson, and he asked if we could chat. He had some questions about selling on Amazon, but he also posed the question, "Why not host your own show?"

Despite my love for the idea, all the doubts came storming in again. When the floodgates of doubt poured in, my major lack of tech skills was the first thing I thought of.

"I can't host my own show," I said. "I don't know how. Who will watch? I don't know anyone that would be interested. What will I talk about? Where will I connect with people? How much will it cost?"

Do you see what happened there? I nearly gave up before I started. But I didn't.

Instead, with the help of Rob, who became my co-host for a time, I decided to launch the show on my birthday. We sent invites among other Facebook groups and, do or die, launched the show. My stomach churned with nerves for the first few minutes, but as we started talking, it all fell away. My love for helping others with the things I'd learned was stronger than the fear. Thirty-three live viewers attended the one-hour show.

That felt like a win.

I knew from that first show that this was what I was meant to do. The call and privilege of sharing my knowledge settled deep inside. "You mean I get to talk for a living and help people and get paid for it?" I cried. "PINCH ME!"

I couldn't have dreamed this life up if I tried. All I did was have hope that things could be better than they were and take the very next step in front of me.

There is always a next step.

Always.

HOW DO WE LEARN TO MOVE PAST FEAR?

Learning to trust the *facts* about a fearful situation and not how we *feel* is the best way to recover from fear. Moving past fear is a skill. Like any new skill, there is a step-by-step formula to follow.

But first, let's talk about facts.

Facts are what can be known. They are true and reliable. Facts are the unchanging, fixed truths that can be known about a situation.

Back to the spiders we go!

What are the facts about spiders? Spiders in Michigan, where I live, are rarely poisonous. The majority don't jump—they run away. Even the slightest chance of my being bitten (and subsequently dying) are extremely small.

Now, what are the *feelings* I have about spiders? Immediate danger. Disgust. Life-threatening panic. Sheer terror.

This is where the rubber meets the road. Are my feelings truth? Let's figure that out.

Even though I *feel* afraid, and my brain signals to run for my life, I am not actually in danger. Feelings are not reliable. The Bible even gives us directions when it comes to our emotions: "He who trusts in his own heart [heart is where our emotions are stored] is a fool," Proverbs 28:26a. Feelings lie to us by giving us the illusion that we can control the situation by running away rather than facing what may come next.

So how do you learn to trust the facts?

The formula to follow is Identification, Exploration, Application. During this process, you will learn to become aware of your fear and be honest about it. We'll explore all the facts, perspectives, and possibilities. The last step is to apply what you have learned by taking—you guessed it—the next small step.

THE PATH TO TRUSTING FACTS

1. Identification:

This is the first step in the formula where you'll be aware of and identify your fear. Answering several questions about the fearful feelings you have will help you identify the main issue and become more aware of it in the future.

Identify Questions:

1. What am I actually feeling?
2. What are my feelings and thoughts based on?
3. Is this holding me back from taking action that can move me in a positive direction?

When you identify where your fear is holding you back, that's when you have the ability to do something about it. This doesn't mean the fear will go away. It means that when you recognize fear and are aware of what it's causing you to feel, you can start making changes toward a more productive set of feelings.

Here is an example of me identifying my own fears. (Please be kind. I am fearful of silly things that often hold me back from taking the next step in my business.)

Example:

My fear: *I refuse to upgrade my phone because I'm afraid of new technology. Learning new tech is too hard and takes me a long time to figure out. I've lost precious pictures and files in the past while trying to upgrade to something new.*

Identify Questions and Answers:

1. **What am I actually feeling?** I am afraid I will fail or lose files and pictures. I'm afraid it will take time away from my business and family trying to figure out a new phone. I don't enjoy new technology. I get easily frustrated with new tech.
2. **What are my feelings and thoughts based on?** I am basing this on previous experiences with new phones. I do things the hard way or lose files because I don't have the right apps or settings. This

always happens to me, and it will again. I am slow at learning how new hardware and software works, and I feel incompetent. I feel stupid because I can't figure things out. I am embarrassed to ask for help. I feel helpless.

3. **Is this holding me back from growing and taking positive action?**
    Yes. I need to be faster and more efficient. I need to speed up what I am doing and gain more time for more important things. I feel it will take too long to learn and I will be just as slow.

Everyone has fear. Whether it seems silly or illogical like spiders or new technology, it still feels very real. Identifying fear may be tricky at first because it can be subtle. It hides behind excuses and procrastination. When we admit we have fear, we aren't surrendering to weakness. We're admitting we're human. Fear means we care about the result or the impact it will make on others.

If we *didn't* care, we wouldn't be afraid.

Fear is a sign that you care deeply about what you are doing. That is a good thing if we can move past it into action.

Step Small 2: Using the above questions, identify one of your fears in business.

2. Exploration

Now that we've identified the feelings and fears, we can begin to explore all the facts. Fact-finding can help us make better decisions based on what is true instead of how we feel.

Exploration Questions:

- What is true about the situation I am facing?
- What is the worst thing that could happen if I try this? (Will I die, though?)
- What are the positive outcomes if I attempt this?

Here are some of my own personal answers. As you practice this exercise, fear will begin to take a backseat to the facts.

Example Exploration Questions:

- **What is true about the situation I'm facing?** People get new phones and new tech every day. I am not alone. Training is available. It will take time to figure it out. There are people and videos that can help me. Everything I need to learn is available to me.
- **What is the worst thing that could happen if I try this?** The worst thing would be losing all pictures, apps, files, contacts, and have to start over. Would I die? No. Could I survive? Yes. I would be annoyed, but I would live.
- **What are the positive outcomes if I attempt this?** The best thing would be that it would be a smooth, easy transition, everything would transfer with a push of a button, and there would be very few changes I need to learn. I would become faster and more efficient in life by upgrading to technology that will serve me better and save time in the long run.

Whew, that was harder than I thought. In fact, I put off writing this chapter because of my fear. But now that I've written it out, I've found it easier to work through my worries of feeling dumb and incompetent.

Step Small 3: Explore the fear you identified in the last section by answering the questions.

3. Application

After the exploration questions, new facts and truths will be revealed. You should feel more equipped to handle the situation. By this point, you may have discovered many new facts about your situation. You've mentally walked yourself through the options, where to find help, worst-case scenarios, and best-case scenarios. You've unearthed the reality of what can happen if you make a change.

Now it's time to apply what you've learned and turn it into action.

Application Questions:

- What have I learned about the facts I have gathered?
- How will my life change if I attempt this despite what I am feeling?
- What is one step I can take right now to get closer to my goal of conquering this?

Example Application Questions:

- **What have I learned about the facts I have gathered?** I learned I'm not alone, and there are ways to get help. The more help I ask for, the faster I will learn. I do not have to do it all myself.
- **How will my life change if I attempt this despite what I am feeling?** I will not drop calls, miss important messages, nor have to carry a clunky charger around because my battery only lasts two hours. I will learn new skills and become more efficient. I will be proud of myself for doing something hard and scary. I will be faster and have a fancy new phone that can do far more with than my current one.
- **What is one small step I can take right now to get closer to my goal of conquering this?** I can make a list of apps, files, and contacts just in case something goes wrong. I can watch instructional videos before I purchase a new device. I can set up an appointment with someone to show me how to do more advanced things with my new technology.

Ok, ok. I know that last one was three small steps, but after doing all this, I feel much more confident about getting a new phone.

I still don't like the idea, but now I feel much better about it because I have facts to rely on.

Now, I am handing over the reins to you. It's time to be brave.

Dig deep inside, and take a good long look at the fears that are holding you back. This is an intimidating step but an important one for your business. Once you understand what is holding you back, you can take small steps to move forward.

Step Small 4: Answer the application questions regarding the fear you identified.

FROM FAILURE TO CONFIDENCE

Meet Janie.

Janie is a client I had a few years ago. She was terrified to continue in her business—and rightfully so. Janie learned about the Amazon business model after seeing an advertisement for a program that promised to find her pallets of brand-new inventory with excellent rankings that she could sell in her Amazon store. She wasn't confident in her ability to find fast-selling products, so this sounded like an amazing opportunity for her to jumpstart her business.

Many promises were made about the quality of the products and great sell-through rate. Testimonials told stories of how others had made thousands of dollars by purchasing pallets from this company. Best of all—the pallet came with a manifested list (a full list of each product included in the shipment), sales rankings, average selling prices, and average profit margins. Based on the testimonials, reviews, and information, she bought the pallet of inventory.

When the pallet arrived, it seemed exactly as described. Some items were unsellable due to damaged boxes, but she could try to sell them someplace else. She did the work to send the items in to

Amazon. Then . . . crickets. Turns out the provided manifest was completely falsified. The brand names and products matched the manifested list, but the Amazon sales rankings and average selling prices were completely made up. These are key factors in determining which products sell well on Amazon and which ones don't.

Some of the items had never sold on Amazon at all.

Janie was devastated by her huge mistake. She should have double-checked every item on the manifest before making a purchase. She trusted them and got burned. She never sold a single item from that pallet and lost thousands of dollars.

Based on this experience, Janie was terrified to invest in her business. She had no confidence in herself anymore. When I offered to help, she was reluctant. She didn't know who she could trust. She didn't want to make more mistakes and had pretty much given up.

On our call, we walked through this fact-based (instead of fear-based) formula with her situation and talked through each question. She realized that she made mistakes . . . but she survived. Her fear was real, but she was in control of what happened next.

After digging deep, she realized she lacked the confidence to find products for her Amazon store because she'd tried to take a shortcut instead of learning how to make good buying decisions on her own.

Her next small step was to learn how to choose products for herself. She took our course on how to research and find good-selling products, and within six months she was back on her feet. She'd made two times what that original pallet cost her. She took a step. She made a change. She still struggles with fear when it comes to trusting others, but now she has more confidence in herself and her ability to find the right products to sell.

Like Janie, we'll need to practice quizzing ourselves over and over again as we face new fears. As we do this, we *will* discover new facts that will give us the confidence we need to take the next small step. When we continue to take small steps (even while feeling fear), we get better at trusting the facts, not the feelings.

LIMITING BELIEFS

What we believe dictates how we act.

If we continue to embrace fear, those thoughts and feelings will limit what we can accomplish. Throughout our lives, we learn many belief systems. Some serve us well, and some don't. As a child, we didn't have a choice on what belief systems we adopted—we were surviving, living, and trusting what we were taught. But one of the greatest things about being an adult is the ability to make our own choices. We can choose to do things completely different than our parents. Guess what?

That is perfectly ok.

Whoever raised you did what they thought was best for you, but that doesn't mean you have to embrace *everything* they taught you.

No matter where we originate, we all have limiting beliefs swimming in our heads, feeding us lies. Many are subtle whispers; others are megaphones with bright red stop signs. I shared a few with you earlier when I spoke about the speaker application I deleted.

Here are a few more:

> *"I'm going to fail."*
> *"I'm not good enough."*
> *"I don't have enough experience."*
> *"I am not as good as her."*
> *"I'm too old to start something new."*
> *"I'm not educated."*
> *"I'm just a mom."*

"I'm not business savvy."

"I don't know how."

"I don't have a degree."

"I can't."

"I couldn't do that."

"I'm not ready."

"I don't have enough time."

"I can't handle rejection."

"They'll judge me."

"No one will take me seriously."

It's unfortunate that I could write an entire chapter of negative thoughts that we allow in our heads. You are not alone! Everyone has these thoughts. They are the wall standing between you and your IAPW. Every time you surrender to one of these thoughts, you step away from your true desire. These thoughts, doubts, and limiting beliefs will always linger. What you do with them is what will make the difference.

Ultimately, what separates successful people from scared people is action. Throughout this entire book, you have action steps given to you (and more in the back!). It's up to you to separate yourself from your fear and become the confident, successful woman waiting on the other side. There are no shortages of action steps in this book. Your excuses won't stand.

It's time for action.

Step Small 5: Make a list of the limiting beliefs you carry around. These could have come from other people in your life, your child-hood, or may be self-imposed. Nothing is too big or too small. Get it all out there. Be honest with yourself. (Don't worry—no one's looking and no one's judging.)

Example: *Only people with a college degree can make a six-figure income. (From my childhood.) Moms shouldn't work outside the home. (Some women in my life.) I can't handle being turned down. (People-pleaser.) I need more training before I get started. No one will care about what I want to offer. Too many other women are doing what I am doing, etc.*

FLIP THE SCRIPT

Now we're going to take this one step further. Identifying the limiting beliefs isn't enough. We need to try out a new script.

The tired, worn, unhealthy script you've played over and over in your mind doesn't have to remain there. Swap those limiting beliefs for a healthier version, and begin to embrace new truths. Doing this will take time and practice.

Trust me; it's well worth it.

I call this flipping the script. The old thoughts have been there for decades and are the default in our brain. We need to retrain our brain to replace the old script with a new one.

Here are some new thoughts to try on:

Old Script: "I'm going to fail."
New Script: "I cannot fail if I learn from my attempts. Failure is a temporary setback. Failure is a bruise, not a tattoo."

Old Script: "I'm not good enough."
New Script: "I don't have to be the best in order to share my ideas. I just need to be one step ahead of the person I am teaching. I'm enough."

Old Script: "I don't have experience."
New Script: "I give myself permission to be a beginner. I have the courage to try."

Old Script: "I am not as good as her."
New Script: "I am a unique individual with thoughts and ideas to share with the world. Comparison is the thief of joy. I will do my best every day to be the best version of myself without comparing myself to others."

Old Script: "I'm too old to start something new."
New Script: "I have lived a longer life. It gives me a unique perspective and years of experience. God is not done with me until I die. There is plenty of time to pursue new things."

Old Script: "I'm just a mom."
New Script: "I am a woman with special gifts and talents. Being a mom is only one piece of who I am. Moms are excellent at wearing many hats. I have learned many skills in motherhood that will apply to business."

Old Script: "I don't have enough time."
New Script: "I will make time for what is most important to me and eliminate things that don't align with my IAPW."

Old Script: "They'll judge me."
New Script: "No one's opinion will ever pay me money. I am doing great work that will impact the world."

There is always a way to change the way we think. Practicing these new beliefs and resetting your default to a more positive mindset will allow you to explore new adventures on the other side of fear. I like to say *new hope, new action.* Based on your facts, your research, and your own fresh ideas, you arrive at a new hope. A hope that life can change.

Now, it's time to really dig deep with our next Step Small.

Step Small 6: When we trust the facts and not our feelings, we begin to see things more clearly. Pick three of your limiting beliefs that are not in alignment with your IAPW. Design a new hope for that limiting belief. Back it up with research, a true story, or other facts.

Example 1: *Moms should stay home with their kids. Working while your children are young will distract you from being a good parent.*

Research: *According to a Harvard researcher, kids of working moms are just as happy as other children with stay-at-home moms. Another Harvard Business school article states children who have working mothers tend to earn higher wages, have more quality time with parents, and are more independent than kids whose moms stayed at home.*

New truth: It's most likely that my children won't resent me for working. Research supports that expectation. In fact, my children will be more inclined to do the same and follow in my footsteps. I am contributing to my family financially and modeling good work ethics and independence for my children. Feeling guilty that I am not with them all day is a choice that I don't have to make. They will love me no matter what.

Example 2: *I assumed that because I didn't finish college and get a degree, I'd always live paycheck-to-paycheck and never have anything more than basic necessities.*

Research: *Kristin Ostrander built a seven-figure online e-commerce business and a six-figure online education and e-course business without a college degree. She did this while staying home with her children. New research shows that skills are more important and more valuable than degrees in many fields.*

New truth: Millions of people start and create businesses—and get great paying jobs—without degrees. I can do the same. I am capable of learning and growing my income potential outside of college.

Step Small 7: New hope, new action. Now that you know new truths are possible, it's time to take one small action step in the direction of your new truth. Make a list of tasks that will move you closer to your dream and further from fear.

Example: *With my new belief, I know I don't have to feel guilty about being separated from my children. I would like to hire a babysitter or a daycare center a few times a week to give me more time to work on my business.*

Example: *It's possible for me to increase my income without a college degree. I will make a list of all the skills I have or could learn and research opportunities to earn income with those skills.*

STEP SMALLS IN THIS CHAPTER:

1. Take sixty seconds and write as many fears as you can think of. Remember that no one is looking or judging. Be real with yourself.
2. Using the above questions, identify one of your fears in business.
3. Explore the fear you identified in the last section by answering the questions.
4. Answer the application questions regarding the fear you identified.
5. Make a list of the limiting beliefs you carry around.
6. Pick three of your limiting beliefs that are not in alignment with your IAPW. Design a new hope for that limiting belief. Back it up with research, a true story, or other facts.
7. Make a list of tasks that will move you closer to your dream and further from fear.

Chapter 5

OWN YOUR OWNERSHIP

Step Small 1: Decide you are a business owner.

When I started selling products online, it never occurred to me that I was running a business.

I was just a stay-at-home-mom trying to earn a few bucks. After all, I sold children's clothing, toys, and a few books, making a few hundred dollars a week here and there. *Real* businesses made much more than that. They usually had employees and their own building.

Not me.

The term entrepreneur was never a part of my vocabulary. My dad was a working-class guy who came from a very poor family. He struggled with ADD and hated school. He needed to be busy with his hands, definitely not sitting behind a desk. He encouraged me to go to college so that I didn't have to struggle like he did his whole life.

And I did go to college. For two years.

After taking all the required courses, I still couldn't pick a major. At eighteen years old, I had no idea what I wanted to do for the rest of my life because no career appealed to me at that time. My father believed a better education would yield a better life.

I agreed with him . . . but not in the traditional way.

COLLEGE DROPOUT

I believe in education and am a self-proclaimed education addict. The problem was college wasn't teaching me anything I was interested in. Unless I am going into something scientific, why the heck do I need to take biology?

Can I get an amen?

What I learned on my own was far more relevant than anything I learned in school. The school of hard knocks taught me about financial irresponsibility, car repossession, and bankruptcy. I learned how to feed a family of five on $30 a week. I have perfected the $20 date night. I learned how to make money while nursing a baby. Unfortunately, I also learned a limiting belief that life was never fair, and you may have to work harder than others to get the same results.

One day during a self-education study session on online selling, I was reading through a seller forum. Other online sellers were getting products for better prices than I was, and I wanted to know how. That's when I stumbled on an intriguing concept. Another seller was talking about the benefits of a registered business. *Registered business?* I thought. *Surely that isn't me. I don't have a business. I just sell stuff online. Real businesses have buildings and employees and big, huge copy machines. Nope. That definitely isn't me.*

Instead of dismissing it entirely, though, I read farther. That's when I found a new word.

Entrepreneur.

Do you know how long it took me to learn to spell that? Let's not go into it. Anyway, the way the forum sellers were using that word gave me the general idea of what it meant. An entrepreneur is someone who owns a business.

Again, not me.

Still, I had to keep investigating. Google to the rescue! My search results revealed more than I expected, such as the following definition:

> *An entrepreneur is a person who organizes and operates a business, taking on greater than normal financial risks in order to do so.*[2]

---

2 https://www.shopify.com/blog/117049413-what-exactly-is-an-entrepreneur-and-how-do-you-become-one-today

Ok, ok. That *might* be me, but I don't have a business. I just sell stuff online. But just to be sure, I learn more.

Back to Google.

What is business? I typed into the search engine.

Business is the practice of making one's living by engaging in commerce.[3]

Huh. Commerce. I pressed on.

What is commerce? I asked next.

The activity of buying and selling . . .[4]

See? Education is happening right here and now. You're welcome.

According to these definitions, my "little Amazon/eBay store" was a real, legitimate business. My world stopped. A light bulb went off.

I was an entrepreneur.

Thoughts flooded my mind. Thoughts I'd never had before. Dreams. Big ones. Dreams I didn't know were in there. I was sitting in my office, and I stood up to catch my breath. This was a whole new concept for me. I didn't just sell stuff online. I was *making my living by engaging in commerce.*

"I am a business owner and entrepreneur," I whispered to myself. I wanted it to really sink in because deep in my soul I knew this small step was a turning point.

Going to college and having a high-level corporate job wasn't required to run a business. I didn't need those to find financial freedom. I didn't need a degree to run a business; I was already doing it! All I needed to do was educate myself on how to grow—and more importantly—give myself permission to dream.

To dream so big my brain couldn't take it.

After all, how would I know where I wanted to take my *business*

---

3 https://www.encyclopedia.com/social-sciences-and-law/economics-business-and-labor/economics-terms-and-concepts/business-0

4 https://en.oxforddictionaries.com/definition/us/commerce

if I didn't dream about it? I took the time to really accept and own this new concept.

I am a business owner.

Own Your Ownership

Have you ever minimized your business?

Have you ever felt like you had *this little thing you were doing* but didn't elevate it to the status it deserved?

I am here to give you the good news. You are indeed an entrepreneur and a business owner! Congratulations. You have just been promoted. Just kidding, you've always been the CEO. But now is the time to give yourself permission to recognize, acknowledge, and accept it.

Yes, you are the owner.

The CEO.

Ponder that for a second. Let it sink in and fill your soul.

You make all the decisions and control the direction. You decide what your schedule will be. This flexibility and freedom is something most people dream about! It's the reason many people start businesses. This is what you wanted, isn't it?

Ownership.

Once I allowed the truth of being a real business owner to settle into my mind, I began to feel both empowered and scared. Empowered because I knew I had something that could be bigger than I'd imagined. Scared because of the weight and pressure of such a massive responsibility. Up until this point, I was just playing it by ear. I didn't think of myself as an owner. It felt like a hobby that paid me to participate.

When I internalized the fact that I was running a business, I knew I needed to make a shift in how I thought about it. I began to think like an owner instead of a hobbyist. I had already shifted into a fully-functional, tax-paying, income-earning business.

I had better start treating it that way.

Step Small 2: Visualize. Visualize yourself as the owner and organizer of a company who deals in goods or services that people love. Visualize yourself in a meeting delegating important tasks to others who are more than happy to do them for you. Whisper it, write it down, or shout it from the rooftops.

Boss.

CEO.

Owner.

Head Honcho.

Friend, this is already you. Own it.

This is a small step and a very important one. Why? Believing and owning that thought will make all the difference in how you operate.

If you describe your business as *this little eBay store* or a *small side hustle,* then that's all it will ever be. Owning it isn't about how big your business is or how much you earn. It's a mindset shift that will empower you to think differently about what you are doing. Your actions follow your thoughts.

If you imagine yourself sitting behind a big corner office while your people come in for your final approval on projects, it will help you hold your head up higher. If you believe you are the capable decision-maker, you will naturally make better decisions. Even if you're really only working from the card table of your guest bedroom, you are the CEO of your business.

Let that take root in your soul.

Think about how these two examples sound to you.

You're at a party, and the conversation comes turns to what you do for a living. What sounds better?

"I have a little Amazon store where I sell kids stuff."

Or . . .

"I am the founder and CEO of an online business specializing in children's items."

Before you throw me under the bus for using fancier words, hear me out. Repeat the phrase in the first example. Really. Say it out loud. How do you feel? Do you feel strong and confident? Are you proud to say that out loud? Now, how about the second phrase? Say that out loud. Now how do you feel?

Owning your ownership changes your perspective. It builds your confidence.

As women, we tend to minimize what we're doing. We're afraid of being too boastful. We play down our strengths so we don't appear intimidating or arrogant.

This must stop.

If you want to have all you ever dreamed of, you have to upgrade something besides your minivan.

Upgrade your mind.

You are the owner. Say it. Own it. Believe it.

Step Small 3: Write an empowering statement about your business that you can practice saying. When someone asks, "What do you do?" or "What type of business do you have?" this will be the answer you will feel proud to say. Do not minimize it. Own it.

STEP SMALLS IN THIS CHAPTER:

1. Decide you are a business owner.
2. Visualize yourself as the owner and organizer of a company who deals in goods or services that people love.
3. Write an empowering statement about your business that you can practice saying.

Chapter 6

THE 15-MINUTE HUSTLE

(A special note for non-moms . . . stick with me here. This chapter contains a strategic necessity even if you don't have children.)

Dreaming about your IAPW, constructing your ideal job, and working through fear-ridden obstacles can seem defeating and far off when you are in the trenches of "momming."

When the day-to-day tasks like changing diapers and folding laundry consume your time, it's hard to believe that one day those same little ones will have families of their own. One day they'll cut their own food, and the words, "Mommy, mommy, mommy!" will no longer be heard a hundred times a day.

Still, when you are in that stage of life, you dream.

Just not like one might think.

MOM BOSS LIFE

To a mom of young children, dreams may look a bit different. A dream might be to *actually* dream. A night with six or more hours of uninterrupted sleep would *feel* like a dream! Perhaps a shower that is longer than the five minutes it takes a toddler to smash all the eggs in the fridge (true story)!

When I was a teenager, a commercial featuring a mom chasing messy-faced kids around a chaotic house played often on TV. Then, it would cut to the mom taking a bubble bath in what appears to be a tropical place. A calming voice whispers, "Calgon, take me away!" Then, it snaps back to the view of the mom sniffing a body wash product in a supermarket with three kids in the cart. I didn't get it then.

Now, I totally get it.

What mom on earth has time for Calgon to take her away?

The struggle is REAL!

When your biggest fantasy involves a long, uninterrupted bubble bath and a good night's sleep, who has time to dream bigger? Dreaming bigger seems selfish, silly, and indulgent. The biggest hurdle most mom bosses face is neglecting ourselves. We dismiss our own needs, dreams, and desires for the sake of others.

Sometimes we just can't fit it all in. We often go days or even months without caring for ourselves. (I don't just mean a good long shower. Please don't go months without that!) I mean *truly* nurturing ourselves and our passions.

When we become moms, we often lose a sense of our own identity. Our kids become our life, and everything tends to revolve around them. We care for them, love them, teach them, and spend all of our energy doing so, leaving nothing left for ourselves. Although that seems very noble, it's extremely backward.

Even on airplanes, they tell us to put our own oxygen masks on before we help others!

We need to give ourselves permission to be our own unique selves. Before we had children, we had passions, talents, hobbies, desires. That doesn't go away just because we became a mom. Becoming a mom might change some of those passions and desires, but they don't change who we are inside.

Becoming a mom doesn't change our identity; it enhances it. It's another part of us, not the whole person.

Motherhood is when most women give up on the hopes and dreams they once had. They assume they will spend the next twenty-some-odd years raising amazing humans and that will be their sole purpose and identity. Later, they may decide to pursue other things . . . once the kids are grown.

Friends, this is not the way.

You don't have to wait. You *can* have both, and you can have both *right now.*

How to Fight Mommy Guilt

Imagine what you hope for your own children as they grow up.

Would you ever say to them, "Grow up. Get married. Have children. Put all your hobbies, hopes, and dreams on hold so you can serve them; then, get back to regular life once they're gone."

How sad would that feel?

Even if you love parenting, it's still only one part of you.

Perhaps you'd say something like this instead, "Follow your dreams. Do what you love. Be adventurous. Live, travel, enjoy life. Be safe, be kind. Learn new things; meet new people." So why on earth don't we talk to ourselves like this?

Why do we tell ourselves that everyone else is more important, and we are last in line? Why do we neglect the very things that make us unique for the sake of laundry? Most of us are wired to serve, love, nurture, and protect. We do that for everyone but ourselves.

Friends, this has got to stop!

How can we be our best self to our spouse, our children, and our business if we don't protect the asset that is keeping it all together?

US!

Inside, we feel it's selfish or indulgent to spend time on things that are strictly me-oriented. Like our health, our spiritual needs, and our passions. We just feel *bad*. We think that if we spend time caring for ourselves, we must be neglecting something else. Mommy Guilt is real.

It's time to put on our boxing gloves and start fighting it.

In the last chapter, you learned to *trust the facts, not the feelings*. This can help with Mommy Guilt. Guilt is a *feeling*. We feel bad for not being with the kids all the time, and we feel bad when we are with our kids all the time. It brings us down and is a vicious cycle.

Instead, let's examine the facts.

The facts say that we deeply love our children, and we care for them every day. We give plenty of hugs, read tons of stories, and respond to the, "Mommy, mommy, mommy!" one hundred times a day.

That is love.

Here is the truth: Mommy Guilt will never go away because it proves you care. I call this the *Snuggle, Don't Struggle.*

Let me explain.

If you feel bad for *not* doing something, it's because you care about that thing, or person, or cause. Your guilt will only disappear if you become perfect (HA!) or if you stop caring. Both of which are very unlikely. Instead, *snuggle* with the guilt instead of *struggling* against it. Give it a hug, and thank it for reminding you that you care enough about your kids to feel bad when you aren't constantly meeting their every need.

Then, promise to do one thing (or stop doing one thing) that you've been feeling guilty over. (Like scrolling Pinterest instead of paying attention to the kids, amIright?)

Step Small 1: Do one thing you've been putting off (or stop doing one thing) that you've been feeling guilty about. Follow up with the kids' teacher or (stop) scrolling Instagram instead of playing with Playdoh. (I'm throwing myself under the bus right here!)

PERMISSION TO LIVE

Why do we believe we have to put our lives and dreams on hold to raise children?

The truth is, we don't.

Just in case you need it, I give you permission to live. To dream.

To do whatever it is that lights your soul on fire but that you've been putting off. I give you permission to set a fantastic example of endurance, patience, and grit for those around you.

Because guess what?

We can be good moms *and* good at other things. We can be great business owners *and* great moms. We weren't created to do one thing in life, or even one thing at a time.

Let's get real about perspective here . . .don't forget who is watching. Like it or not, our kids want to copy everything we do. We lead by example, good or bad. What kind of example am I setting for my children if I tell them to do their best, work hard, use their gifts, and dream big, but don't practice these things myself?

Friends, they are watching our every move. If we demonstrate how much joy we find in using our gifts and talents, they will want to do the same. If we show them how important they are (and how important business is), they may follow in our footsteps. They see us for who we really are.

So, what do you want them to see?

THE 15-MINUTE HUSTLE

Getting rid of fear, owning my role as CEO, and shucking off Mommy Guilt sounds fine and dandy when you have the corner office with a view, but the only view I had was messy-faced kids and a living room that would make Mr. Clean cringe.

While attempting to run an online store with small kids, I did the best I could. With two young kids, that was a challenge. My son was a strange version of *Curious George* meets *Dennis the Menace*. Time was not on my side! On any given day I could only grab about 15 minutes before trouble would arise.

Thus, began what I call the *15-Minute Hustle*.

The 15-Minute Hustle was me trying to get everything done in my business *and* in my household. With my four-year-old and one-year-old underfoot, fifteen minutes was about all I had to spare in one sitting. I had to be organized and efficient. I created a master list of tasks that needed to be done and would tick them off one fifteen-minute chunk at a time.

In our book *The 15-Minute Hustle*[5] that my business bestie Amy Feierman and I wrote, we cover this subject in detail. When we see a hole in the schedule or a random window of opportunity while one of the kids is occupied, we grab the list and do the next thing. For the full version of the book and a more in-depth look at how the 15-Minute Hustle strategy works, head over to www.15minutehustle.com.

Here is an example from the book of the things we put on the 15-Minute Hustle list.

Work:

1. Email
2. Customer Service
3. Marketing
4. Client contact
5. Research
6. Writing
7. Social media
8. Design
9. Education

Family:

1. Read to kids
2. Play with them
3. Homework
4. Coloring

---

5 To get your free copy (and more lists!), visit: https://www.15minutehustle.com

5. Hanging out
6. Birthday parties
7. Extracurricular activities

The 15-Minute Hustle helped me accomplish a small pile of dishes, take a few pictures for eBay listings, or make a phone call. The task was short and sweet because that is all the time I had to work with. I cleaned my house, took care of household chores, and worked on my business 15 minutes at a time.

Each task didn't always get done in that 15-minute stretch, but progress is progress no matter how small. I still use this practice fifteen years later because it always works! Even if you have a gigantic task, it can be done one small step at a time.

For the last 15 years, I've 15-Minute-Hustled my way through life. Reading with such a busy schedule is next to impossible! Who has time to sit down and read for an hour with two small children? But 15 minutes could easily be stolen a few times a day. Same with trying to run a home-based business. My eBay and Amazon stores required tasks like taking photos, writing listings, packaging, and shipping. There was no way to get it all done in one sitting. Within a few days, however, I could easily do it in multiple 15-Minute Hustles.

It isn't easy, but it's possible with a list and a plan. This isn't limited to your business either.

You can 15-Minute Hustle your Mom life.

Game of Candyland? 15 minutes.
Swingset outside? 15 minutes.
Coloring or painting? 15 minutes.
Building Lego castles? 15 minutes.
Reading (with or without the kiddos)? 15 minutes.

My friend Christy Wright, business coach and creator of Business Boutique, summed it all up in a few sentences that really stuck with me.

She says, *"No matter where you are, be 100% present. If you are with your kids, be 100% with them. They will feel it. They will know. If you are at work, be 100% present there and do your best while you are there."*

Truth bomb!

How many times have we been glued to our phones while simultaneously playing a game with our kids? Oh my! I've been there.

The great news is that your life doesn't have to be this way. We *can* do both. Allow me to let you in on a little secret: our kids don't need more than fifteen minutes at a time of our undivided attention. They are almost always satisfied with a little facetime that's undistracted, undivided attention.

This isn't the phone-in-hand-eyes-on-the-screen-shirt-tugging while your child pleads, "Mommy, it's your turn!" We are talking about undistracted time. Time where it is just you and them with their dolls, legos, superhero action figures, or whatever else they are into. They just want us.

100% of us.

Another secret: they never care how much you weigh, how clean the house is, or that they had cereal for dinner. They *love* us. They want to be included in what we do, and they want to feel special and important. If we guard our time with them and parent with intent, we will be raising very happy children.

Let's make a promise to ourselves right now.

- Promise that you will not lay aside everything that makes you who you are and use raising kids as your excuse.
- Promise to own that you can be your whole self. Mom,

business owner, musician, artist, writer, lawyer, anything and everything you want all at the same time.

- Promise to believe you can step into your IAPW 15 minutes at a time. It starts right now. You do not have to wait until there is more free time in your life.
- Promise to believe you can be successful with the 15-Minute Hustle. You can build your business or pursue your passion right now. Today. It is important to start stepping closer to your IAPW on a daily basis. 15-Minute Hustles are the key to getting you there.

If nothing else, for fifteen minutes today you can escape to a place that is one step closer to your IAPW.

Just take the very next step.

Step Small 2: Take some time to think about what you have put on hold since becoming a mom. Is that still important to you? If so, what is one step you could take towards that passion?

Step Small 3: If you are still pursuing your passions after becoming a mom, but still find yourself feeling bad about it, try this: Grab a piece of paper, and list the reasons why your hobbies, passions, and work will benefit your children.

Use "I statements" like this:

- I am happy to contribute to the financial success of my family so we can do things we enjoy.
- I love yoga. Working out consistently sets a good example for my children to learn healthy habits.
- I teach music lessons as a passion and for income. It allows me to use my gift of music while earning a living. This shows my children that I can make money doing what I love, and that work can be very enjoyable.

STEP SMALLS IN THIS CHAPTER:

1. Do one thing you've been putting off (or stop doing one thing) that you've been feeling guilty about.
2. Take some time to think about what you have put on hold since becoming a mom. Is that still important to you? If so, what is one step you could take towards that passion?
3. Grab a piece of paper, and list the reasons why your hobbies, passions, and work will benefit your children.

FAKE IT 'TIL YOU MAKE IT

Is Motivation a Myth?

Motivation is defined as *the general desire or willingness of someone to do something, or the reason one has for acting or behaving in a particular way.*[6]

Basically, we act according to what we believe is true. Our reason. Our Big Why. No one ever wakes up and says, "Today, I feel like going to the dentist." You don't just wait for the morning when you *feel* like going to the dentist. You book an appointment that holds you accountable because you know it's important to take care of your teeth. Even though it can be unpleasant, it has to be done.

This is why motivation is a myth.

If we wait to *feel* like doing hard or uncomfortable things, we will never do them. If we continually rely on feelings and emotions to guide our choices, we will never break through to a new place.

When we hear the word *motivation,* most of us have a positive reaction. We think of inspirational videos, quotes, and people who have great success stories. We see someone going after their dreams or training for a marathon, and we think, "Wow. That person is really motivated."

Do you think she stayed on the couch and waited to *feel* like bundling up and running 10 miles in the rain?

Not a chance.

---

6 https://prezi.com/vsgfah4tqbck/human-motivation/

Instead, she made a commitment and a choice. She takes action based on what she *values* in her life, not how she *feels*. If she's running a marathon, fitness and health are something she values, so her action isn't based on how she feels. She's motivated by her ultimate reason and purpose and makes a decision based on that.

Motivation is all about choices.

Life is a Series of Choices

Motivation is a feeling we can't trust. It ebbs and flows depending on mood (especially when Aunt Flo herself is in town). Motivation is about what moves us to action. When we feel like moving, we move. When we don't feel like moving, we don't. We're motivated by what we think will be best for us at a specific moment in time. We make choices based on feelings and instincts. It's a survival instinct to stay alive. To avert danger and find safety.

So, what does this have to do with motivation and choice?

Life is just a series of choices: the good, the bad, and the ugly.

We do exactly what we want to do every single day to feel what we want to feel. We take action based on what we believe will bring us the most satisfaction at any given moment. Even if the choices we make are bad, we still make them based on what we currently want to feel.

Here is an example.

Your toddler is begging for a toy at the store, and he wants it really, really bad. You say *no*. He proceeds to catapult himself onto the floor in a full-blown meltdown. You're embarrassed and give him the toy because that feels better than the judgmental looks from everyone watching.

At that moment, a decision was made based on what would bring the most satisfaction or relief right then.

You weren't thinking of the subsequent tantrums that might arise. Instead, you ultimately believed that giving in felt better than enduring judgmental looks from strangers. You wanted immediate relief regardless of the future consequences.

Ask me how I know?

When my son was little, I had my fair share of shameful scowls. I made the choice to avoid embarrassment sometimes, but the consequences served me up a nice, hot plate of regret when I finally had to deal with the tantrums properly.

Whether you like it or not, all choices will have either positive or negative consequences.

So, what if we still aren't feeling like making the most productive, positive choices?

FAKE IT 'TIL YOU MAKE IT

The same principle applies in business. We are definitely not going to feel like doing things like taxes or firing someone who isn't pulling their weight.

If we are *unmotivated* to take the next step, it's because, ultimately, we believe something in the present moment will bring us more satisfaction than the uncomfortable or hard action for a better future. It's a paradox of instant gratification. We want a result right now to motivate us to keep moving.

Take weight loss. Most of us could make a few more healthy choices these days, right? Sometimes we make a choice that isn't the healthiest one. Cake over apples. Couch over the gym.

Why?

We make choices based on want we want and how we feel that moment instead of what is needed or necessary. The gym is hard work, and cake tastes better than apples. In the name of comfort (and feeling good), we make the easier choice.

Here's the truth. You will never *feel* like doing difficult or uncomfortable things.

We are wired to desire good, comfortable, easy feelings. One of my favorite quotes by a very wise (but unknown source) says, "If you want something you've never had, you've got to do something you've never done." Notice how it says *do* something, not *feel* something?

This is where you *fake it 'til you make it.*

This is where we pretend to feel like doing the hard thing until we build a habit of taking action. Eventually, we will "make it." Eventually, it won't seem so hard when we take action and get better at the very thing that scares us. If we continue the habit of making a choice based on value and commitment (and not based on feelings), that choice gets easier.

Friends I get it. We're emotional beings, but we don't have to be ruled and controlled by our negative emotions.

We can fake it until we *feel* it!

Step Small 1: Review what you value; revisit what you desire; and then, take the next step, even if you don't feel like it.

If you believe your business will improve your family's quality of life and give you an outlet to share your gifts, you'll do the necessary work to accomplish it, regardless of how you feel. Fake the feelings, and take the action. The positive feelings *will* follow because you'll be proud of yourself for moving forward.

It's a beautiful circle once you take the next step.

The end result you desire, the delayed gratification, has to be worth it to you. If you want to run a million-dollar business, the decisions you will be faced with will get harder as you grow. The ultimate satisfaction has to be chosen over the immediate satisfaction, and this takes a shift in mindset.

Remember, if you want to make a better life for yourself, you have to make harder choices. Friends, you have made many hard choices in life. You are capable. You are able. You've been doing it your whole life. Making a change is hard; staying stuck and unfulfilled is hard. Choose your hard.

Talk to yourself. Tell yourself that, eventually, the reward will be more satisfying than staying stuck. Tell yourself the delayed reward is worth the current discomfort.

TELL YOURSELF A DIFFERENT STORY

To shift into the mindset of making harder choices, you need to tell yourself a new story. *I am* statements are a great way to *flip the script* and change the monologue in your head.

Remember earlier when we talked about acting like the CEO you want to become? Practicing positive *I am* statements will help with this. It will mentally empower you to make decisions a top-level business owner would make.

When you're dealing with hard choices, or you just aren't feeling it, try a few of these scripts instead:

- I am the owner and executive decision-maker of this business.
- I built this from the ground up.
- I am learning and growing every day.
- I am capable of making hard choices.
- I have made many hard choices in the past, and I can do it again.
- I can choose to do the important things first, and I will feel so free when I cross them off my list.
- I know this is hard, but I got where I am by doing hard things. I can do this too.

We are extremely rude to ourselves and allow negative thoughts to rule over us way too often. When this happens, you need a defense mechanism. *I am* statements can help you combat that. When doubt and negativity creep in, stop them in their tracks by using *I am* statements. Then, try this next step.

Imagine you are talking to your very best friend.

Would you ever tell your BFF she isn't good enough? That she'll fail or she can't accomplish her goals?

Heck NO we wouldn't!

So, why on earth do we allow these thoughts to take the lead in our decision-making?

When we begin to recognize the battle of doubt and negativity in our mind, we have to acknowledge these thoughts and picture someone we love deeply. Would you say these things to that person? What would you say instead? I bet it would sound a bit more like this:

- I know it is hard, but you can do this. How can I help?
- You've got this. Look how far you've come already.
- You are smart and strong. I've watched you do things harder than this. You'll figure it out.
- You will be so proud of yourself when you take the next step.
- I know it's scary, but you are not alone.

I have never been one to stand in the mirror and recite positive affirmations. It always felt weird and awkward. However, give me a friend who is down and out, and I could speak encouraging words to her forever.

Now, when I am battling feelings of laziness, fear, procrastination, or doubt, I simply picture my best friend. I speak out loud what I would say to her if she were struggling in the same way. Hearing the words come out helps me internalize them and own them for myself.

TAKE CARE OF YOUR BOSS

The CEO of a company appears to be the person who gets the most attention and respect in the workplace. They have a staff; they command the room; and when they speak, other people listen. They protect their most valuable asset. The Boss.

That, my friend, is you.

(I know we covered this a few chapters ago, but I don't expect you to be an expert at owning your ownership yet. Still, we need to get comfortable with it.)

In case you forgot, let's reiterate: *you* are the boss, the most valuable asset.

You need to be cared for and protected.

When we are taking care of little ones and running a business, self-care is always last on the list. It's often the one thing we feel even more guilty about than mommy struggles.

I see you.

I know the struggle is real.

Between a shower and an extra twenty minutes of sleep (this is what dry shampoo is for, right?), it feels like there's no time for you. Three days of unwashed hair doesn't feel great. Date night or putting on makeup? Forget it. We're busy, tired, and overwhelmed. Thinking about a pedicure or an expensive haircut falls to the bottom of the list, otherwise known as the *place where to-dos go to die.*

Let's be real. We don't command the room when we walk in— the kids do. We'd probably give our left arm for even one staff member. We think if we run around like crazy people trying to keep the house clean and the kids occupied, then all will be well.

The truth is, we spend too much energy trying to do things we think we *should* do and end up frazzled and stressed. Guess what? Kids pick up on our tones and body language. They know when we're worried, sad, mad, or stressed, and they will imitate it.

If we want healthy, happy kids, we have to model that. When we take good care of ourselves, we feel more relaxed and energized.

We're able to give our families the best version of ourselves instead of what is left over after *we get everything done.*

Truth moment: there is no such thing as getting everything done. There will always be a list. Put your boss at the top, meaning you.

Here's why.

We make better decisions when we are well-rested and relaxed.

In order to stay motivated to make difficult choices towards your IAPW, you need to be in a healthy frame of mind.

Burning the candle at both ends brings nothing good. How often do we yell or get angry when we're running late? (Um, hello, ME!) You'd hardly find me angry after a massage or a quiet breakfast alone with a book. That would be refreshing and energizing! How good of a decision-maker can you be if your day consisted of leftover crust from the kids' toast, a four-hour night's sleep, and a gallon of coffee?

Friends, you have time for better.

You deserve better.

You will be a better person if you're well-cared-for. You can't wait for someone else to come along and force you to go to bed at a decent hour or eat a healthy lunch. It's your choice. Take care of yourself.

Today.

Step Small 2: When is the last time you really took care of yourself, and what did you do? (Hair salon, hot yoga class, pedicure, Netflix binge, night out with friends, shopping, etc.) Pick one thing from that list, and make an appointment right now to do it again.

Make this a priority. A consistent one. When you are well-cared-for, you will be a happier, more productive person. It will also give you something all to yourself to look forward to.

Here is a list of ways to add self-care to your life.

- Read a book
- Take a nap
- Go outside
- Take a walk
- Paint your nails
- Get a pedicure
- Schedule a massage
- Go shopping
- Meet a friend for coffee or a meal
- Write
- Keep a journal
- Unfollow anyone or anything on social media that causes negative feelings
- Get a new hair or makeup color
- Schedule a hair appointment
- Buy new shoes
- Therapy
- Meditate
- Turn off the news
- Watch a movie
- Hire a sitter for no reason

You can do any of these (or add your own), but as a mom and a boss, you *need* time to take care of yourself. Picture how the most important, powerful people have a secret service or personal entourage to protect them. In your business and in your home, that is YOU. Your secret service is your self-care. You must protect your asset by nurturing it and making sure it is in the best mental, physical, and spiritual shape for top performance and decision-making.

Step Small 3: Chose a few of these, and set them as a calendar appointment for four weeks in a row. The consistency of self-care is key.

Step Smalls in this Chapter:

1. Review what you value; revisit what you desire; and then, take the next step, even if you don't feel like it.
2. Pick one thing from your self-care list, and make an appointment right now to do it again.
3. Chose a few self-care items, and set them as a calendar appointment for four weeks in a row.

Chapter 8

ACCOUNTABILITY IS EVERYTHING

Learning from others with experience is essential for growth.

As we implement new changes, we will inevitably hit roadblocks. To become great at something, you must study and practice. I would love to put a book under my pillow and learn by osmosis, but it doesn't work that way. If we want to take steps toward a life we love, we need to know what those steps are. Educating yourself on how others arrived at a place you'd like to go can be game-changing.

FOLLOW, OBSERVE, PRACTICE

At the pivotal point in my business—when I was shifting from selling on eBay to learning how to sell on Amazon—I needed to be sure this could work as a long-term business.

I searched for Amazon success stories. There weren't many at that time, but I found forums to read and a few groups talking about selling on Amazon. I joined them and read the threads. An online radio show called *FBA Radio with Kat Simpson and Chris Green* caught my attention. Kat Simpson was an e-commerce rockstar, and Chris Green was teaching anyone and everyone who would listen how to sell on a new program Amazon offered called Fulfillment by Amazon (FBA). Amazon did all the order-fulfilling so I didn't have to—and I was super interested!

I tuned in one day, and I couldn't believe what I was hearing. New and applicable information! Their online radio show played in the background while I shipped books into Amazon's warehouse. This is where I learned that I could sell *other* items on Amazon.

Hearing Chris talk about the other things he sold on Amazon

was something I'd never heard of—I clearly hadn't been paying enough attention before then.

This was among the many, many game changers I learned from Chris. He is considered the *Godfather of Arbitrage,* and I will be forever grateful for his willingness to share information with the world.

One time during the radio show, he gave out his phone number for those who had questions. I jotted it down . . . then, let it sit there in fear. I had to gather my thoughts. Was he really serious about taking calls? Was this really his number? Would he answer? I didn't want to waste his time. I didn't want to waste an opportunity to ask someone who was where I wanted to be about his business model.

Guess what? I called him.

He answered.

For over thirty minutes, I asked question after question. He talked about tools to use, resources to read, and about his new book that was coming out soon. He gave me a head start on a few things in the book before it released.

From then on, if he was talking, I was listening. If he was writing, I was reading. He was where I wanted to be, so I took his advice. As a direct result, my business took a brand-new direction. It grew ten times bigger in a short period of time. In a few months, I went from making $100 a month on books to making $1,000 by expanding into a new business model. By observing, following, and practicing what he said, I grew my business exponentially.

If you want to grow, you need to learn and practice new skills. For that, you need to lean on someone else.

Step Small 1: Find someone who has success doing what you are doing, and learn from them. Follow them on social media, read, watch, or listen to their content, and put it into practice. Glean one small thing, and make a plan to practice it.

Get a Mentor, Coach, or Accountability Partner

Starting (or running) a business isn't easy.

It takes work. Sometimes, you just don't feel like doing it. I've been there a million times. Binge-watching Netflix has won the battle more times than I'd like to admit. I put the *pro* in procrastination. But one thing pushes me off the couch and into action every time.

My accountability partner.

Or should I say partners? I admit it. I have several accountability partners and for different purposes.

Friends, you need someone else to provide the words of encouragement, or a kick in the butt, to get you going.

Sometimes, it takes a force outside of yourself to take that next step. Getting started is the majority of the battle. Once you show up and get started, you might as well do it. Otherwise, it's just wasted time, effort, money, or worse: all three. If I told my friend I'm going to meet her at the gym, I'm gonna show up. If I'm heading there alone, I will likely blow it off.

That is accountability at work.

What is Accountability?

Accountability is all about being held to your word. It requires giving an account for your time, energy, and money.

Accountability has two parts: internal discipline and external support. Accepting responsibility for your results is important as internal discipline, but it's not enough to sustain you. You need external support from an outside force to keep you moving.

Have you ever heard the phrase *no one is an island*? No great empire was ever built alone. There's a reason for that. Our DNA is designed to push us to connect with others. We need other people's input, feedback, direction, and ideas. We need someone to help us follow through on commitments, meet deadlines, and bring our pity parties to an end.

Accountability is a proven performance enhancer. If you have goals, accountability will get you there faster. This has been proven by hundreds of psychological tests spanning sixty years. The most famous example is the Hawthorne effect, also known as *The Observer Effect,* which states that you'll do a better job when someone is watching you perform a task. The term *Hawthorne Effect* was coined by Henry A. Landsberger in 1950 when he was analyzing experiments conducted in the 1920s at Hawthorne Works, a Western Electric factory near Chicago.[7]

The factory commissioned the study to see if workers would be more productive in higher or lower levels of light. The study showed that no matter what variable changed, the workers' performance increased simply because they were being watched. Productivity improved when the study began and slowed when it ended. In the end, the researchers concluded that the workers' increase in productivity was the direct result of being watched.

Besides the increase in productivity, there are also other major benefits for accountability:

1. Access to constructive feedback on your ideas.
2. Help in meeting deadlines.
3. A sense that someone else is walking the road with you.
4. Greater focus.
5. Faster recovery from mistakes.

ACCOUNTABILITY IN MY BUSINESS

Speaking of conquering a goal with accountability, here is how I've been able to push past hard things to get to where I am today.

Amy.

---

7 McCambridge, Jim et al. "Systematic review of the Hawthorne effect: new concepts are needed to study research participation effects" Journal of clinical epidemiology vol. 67,3 (2014): 267-77.

She and I have been accountability partners (and biz besties) for four years now. I am terrible at tech; she is a tech goddess. When things get tough, and I want to quit, she forces me to walk through the hard things. Like syncing Dropbox and transferring files to the cloud. (Don't judge!) She cares about my success and won't let me off the hook when I get lazy or scared. When I'm stuck, she gives me a dose of my own medicine. She reminds me I have the energy to tackle one 15-Minute Hustle, and then, she goes the extra mile and suggests a few steps to take. Oftentimes, taking one of those steps catapults me into doing more. Getting started is the majority of the battle.

Here are a few Step Smalls she's given me:

1. Write for three minutes.
2. Delete ten emails.
3. Upload one audio file to the correct Dropbox folder.

(See how easy Step Smalls can be?)

In fact, this book would not exist without the gentle but persistent nudging from Amy.

Many times, I would text her saying I was stuck and had writer's block or complain about my lack of energy. I wanted to push the book to the back burner and make other projects a priority (which I did for seven months). Being keenly aware of my goals, Amy wasn't afraid to hold me to my word or force me to take action.

Because of Amy's persistence, I met my writing coach and added an extra layer of accountability. Between the two of them, I had the support I needed to finally get these words into the world. There is no way I could have done this on my own. I tried! The book got pushed to the side again and again. I needed to be open enough to admit I needed help.

Once I surrendered, I got all the help I needed to accomplish my goal.

The Sexiest Words in the World

When it comes to accountability, it's not—you guessed it—all sunshine and rainbows. We need accountability because this growth stuff is hard, often uncomfortable, and scary. Let's be real. No one needs to check on us to see if we've caught up on the latest episode of our favorite show

This Is Us, anyone?

In reality, the difficult tasks we tend to push off are the things that need to be addressed with accountability. This is where the sexiest words in the world come in. Now, I know this is a business book, but come on, friends.

I can use the word *sexy,* right?

I'm not talking about scandalous pillow talk here. I'm talking about the most powerful words you can speak that show someone how much you care.

And the Oscar goes to . . .

"How can I help you?"

Why are these words so sexy? When you hear them, they mean so much more than five little words. When someone offers to help you, they're saying, *I care about you. I see you need help. I am offering you the most precious commodity on earth—my time. I want you to feel more comfortable. How can I ease the stress or burden you are facing?*

WHOA!

Can you imagine how revolutionary it would be if our spouse walked in every day and instead of asking, "How was your day?" they said, "How can I help you?" (Or if *we* did that for them?) Come on! We're dreaming big here, right? I'm adding this to my IAPW right now.

These powerful words are the ultimate accountability phrase. Asking this question can sum up so much.

When you see someone you love struggling, ask them how you can help. When you are struggling, be prepared to answer how *you* can be helped.

Who Can Keep You Accountable?

You need someone who isn't going to sugarcoat your situation and say, "That's really nice."

Someone who is going to push back and make you think, inspire you to put in more effort, and push you out of your comfort zone. This person doesn't need to be in your field of business. It's better if they aren't someone you're really close with.

Close friends or family tend to be more passive. While that feels nice, it won't get us to our IAPW any faster. Amazing things rarely happen in your comfort zone. To stretch and grow we need to step outside our comfort. An accountability partner is a way to be supported while taking that step outside what we're comfortable with.

Finding a person who will be a good fit isn't always easy, however.

Before you start looking for the *who*, let's talk about what you should expect from this person.

Traits of a Great Accountability Partner

They will:

- Be your biggest cheerleader.
- Challenge you to make what seems impossible possible.
- Celebrate every milestone on your journey, no matter how small.
- Make sure your goal remains a priority.
- Prove that you don't have to go it alone.
- Ask questions.
- Communicate with you consistently.

- Be diligent about checking in.
- Provide feedback and support for your projects
- Not let you off the hook when you slack.

Looking for someone who can help you work towards your goals can seem overwhelming. Maybe you are an introvert, shy, or really don't know anyone. I hear you naysayers saying, "I'll just keep myself accountable."

How well is that working for you right now?

Are you continually setting and crushing your goals?

Are you where you want to be?

Are you walking down your IAPW path and truly enjoying your job, business, and life?

Before you dismiss the idea, remember this: top athletes in the world have coaches. Most professional and prominent entrepreneurs consult mentors, hire coaches, and have accountability in their lives.

Know any of these names?

Mark Zuckerberg, the founder and CEO of Facebook, was mentored by Steve Jobs of Apple Inc. Maya Angelou, a celebrated author and poet, mentored Oprah. Oprah said Maya helped guide her through significant milestones in her life and stated she doesn't think anyone in this world makes it without having a great mentor. How about Sally Ride, the first American woman in space? Her graduate school professor, Dr. Arthur Walker, was her lifelong mentor and instilled confidence in her that allowed her to follow her dreams.

Hiring a coach may be the best way to learn what you need to fast-track your success. This is one of the only things I would advise as a shortcut. It will greatly reduce the time it takes you to get you where you want to go. People with accountability perform better and achieve goals faster. I know it can be difficult, but there are many ways to connect with people in non-intimidating ways.

Step Small 2: Begin your search for an accountability partner. Make a list of potential mentors, coaches, or accountability partners.

Step Small 3: Contact one of them.

Here are a few places to look to get you started:

- Facebook groups
- Church
- Mentors
- Local meetup groups (look at meetup.com)
- Personal contacts
- Networking events
- Conferences
- Anything associated with your brand or field of business

Step Smalls in this Chapter:

1. Find someone who has success doing what you are doing, and learn from them. Follow them on social media, read, watch, or listen to their content, and put it into practice. Glean one small thing, and make a plan to practice it.
2. Begin your search for an accountability partner. Make a list of potential mentors, coaches, or accountability partners.
3. Contact one of them.

Chapter 9

GETTING HELP

By now, you've created your IAPW, acquired new insight on how to process fear, and uncovered your potential dream job. You know where you'd like to go, how to use the 15-Minute Hustle to get there, and how to find an accountability partner.

Now I'm going to challenge you even further. Tough love, right?

Are you ready to get closer to your IAPW? If so, there's something you should embrace sooner than later.

You can't do it alone.

No One Is an Island

If you want to change and grow and make big things happen, you'll need help. I'm not just talking about a coach or mentor. No, I'm talking real, practical help. Employees, laborers, admins, housekeepers, virtual assistants, babysitters, etc.

Before you skip to the next section because you think you aren't even close to being ready to hire someone, I want to challenge your belief system once again. This will more than likely redirect you back to Chapter Four, where we discussed fear, and Chapter Six on Mommy Guilt.

For now, let's play a game. A mind-reading game. Are you with me? Yes. I, Kristin, am going to read your mind. (I bet you didn't know I could do that.)

When I tell you that you may have to hire employees to get your IAPW, what are you thinking?

Wait!

This is the part where I read your mind. You're thinking:

- "I am not even sure what I need the most help with."
- "I don't know where to look."
- "I don't know how."
- "Where will I find someone who can do what I do as well as I can?" (Control freak, anyone?)
- "I don't think I will ever have enough money to pay someone to help me."
- "What if I find someone who isn't great, and I have to fire them?"
- "I don't know how to teach someone how to help me."
- "I am so unorganized. How can I manage someone else?"

Did I come close?

Friends, I have said all of these things. I have had the same fears, worries, and doubts. I once worked alone. The slowest growth period I ever had was when I was all alone with no mentor, no employees, and no clear direction. I never thought I could move much faster and more efficiently if I had someone to help me.

The first time I entertained the thought of getting help, I was doing double-duty. By day I was a domestic diva, taking care of kids, cleaning, managing the household, and only working on business in 15-Minute Hustles. By night, I was staying up until two or three in the morning, trying to get everything done when everyone was asleep. It's normal! When you're first starting out, you *can* manage all the things.

But as your business grows, so do your responsibilities.

The sooner you embrace that you can't do this alone, the better off you'll be.

The great news is you already know how to hire people. You've hired many specialists already. Have you ever had a mechanic work on your car? A landscaping service? Dry cleaner? How about a painter, an accountant, or a plumber? A babysitter?

Hiring help is easier than you think.

When you hire a babysitter or select a daycare, you have expectations and a certain level of trust. You know what you want, a price you can pay, and a list of special instructions. This is hiring help. This is the beginning of your team.

The first things I suggest you hire out aren't business related. Anything that takes up time that could be used for a greater purpose is worth outsourcing. For starters, when my business was growing bigger than my 15-Minute Hustles would allow, I hired a babysitter a few times a week.

As my business continued to grow, I had two options:

I could work more and more hours, feeling stressed out and overwhelmed.

I could hire help.

I went a bit beyond ordinary help and welcomed a full-time 50/50 partner.

This woman noticed my success and loved that I was *shopping* for a living. At that time, my business model on Amazon was retail arbitrage, where I'd buy from retail store shelves and resell the items on Amazon for a profit. I really *was* shopping for a living! This wonderful lady was working at a job she dreaded. Every day when it was time to go to work, she wanted to quit. Although she'd been with the same company for nearly twenty years, the job was physically demanding, with afternoon and evening shifts from 4:00 pm until midnight.

As a single mom of older teens—this was *not* when she wanted to be away from home.

This partner is my mother.

My First Partner

The timing was perfect.

I desperately needed help. I trusted her and wanted nothing

more than for her to do something she loved and get away from the job she dreaded. Plus, it would mean I could spend more time with her, and that was the best part!

This wasn't all sunshine and rainbows though.

The transition meant that in an instant, I would take a 50% pay cut. It also meant I had to become a full-blown teacher because she was new to the business. She had to learn everything. Which meant I had to teach her, and I was fairly new to teaching. I had never had to explain and demonstrate every action I took in my business before. Not just the *actions,* but the reasons why I did them. She was the absolute best student and is now better at most of these things than me.

Listen, I understand that these circumstances are special, but there's more to this. My accountability partner, Amy, eventually turned into my business partner through a very unique experience.

Most people assume Amy and I have been friends for our entire lives, but we actually met online four years ago and became instant friends. She was reaching out for help in her business, and our unique perspectives really drove us together. But guess what? Learning to mesh with one another's differences took time and effort.

I'm going to be honest here—taking on a partner has been mostly sunshine and rainbows, but it's also required consistent effort to accommodate our differences. Despite our common goals and values, our execution is often very different. This is how a true partnership should be.

Practice and commitment.

Finding, training, and paying someone new in your business is a scary thing. Letting go of control is difficult because all of the *what-ifs* and *yeah-buts* flood our mind. This is where we have to get back to the entire purpose of this book.

Your next small step.

You don't have to draft a fully-functional-human-resources-style-employee-handbook before you hire help. Decide what you need the most help with, and hire someone to do that task.

Step Small 1: Make a list of small and big things (both domestic and business tasks) you can hire out. Get crazy here . . . think IAPW style. Here is my IAPW hire: I would hire out grocery shopping, food prep, and cooking.

You don't need to hire someone who can do *all the things*. There are some magical unicorns that have every skill you will eventually need . . . but they're probably not in your price range right now.

You don't have to have just one person. It's ok to hire different specialists. You wouldn't ask your babysitter to fix your bathtub, or your dry cleaner to mow your lawn. You won't be asking your bookkeeper to morph into your social media manager (unless of course, she is one of the unicorns we mentioned).

If you want to grow your dream business, you'll need a team.

Just not all at once.

When mom and I partnered, we eventually hired many others and have recently added more permanent team members. I started alone and took small steps to get there. Then, I took additional steps from there to where I am today.

Small steps to big dreams.

After ten years, I have a partner, a virtual assistant, an administrative assistant, and a full support team at the warehouse prep center we use to handle all our inventory. Without everyone on this team, $1.2 million in yearly revenue would never be possible.

Step Small 2: You can hire out nearly anything. Whatever it is you need, narrow down to one thing, and complete the following process before moving on to something else. What you need to focus on in order to narrow down the list is to ask yourself these three questions:

1. What tasks currently bring me the most stress?
2. What will give me the most relief at the moment?
3. What will free up my time in such a way that I can focus on doing the most important things in business and life?

By taking this step, you should have the answer to where you need to start. If hiring a babysitter a few times a week will bring you the most relief, start there. If hiring a housekeeper will help you feel less stressed and create more time to spend in your business (and with your kids), start there.

Know Where You Need Help

Knowing what you need help with is just the beginning. We're stepping small here, so hang in there.

First, we're going to discuss a few steps to take *before* you look for your new hire.

1. Create Training Documents, Processes, and Videos

We don't have to train lawn care or housekeeping professionals, but we can set expectations at the beginning. They'll expect you to tell them how you want things done and when. If you'd like help with something more specific to your business, you'll need to document all the steps to complete the tasks the way *you* desire them to be done.

Start by writing down what needs to be taught to that new person. Let's start with my grocery shopping example.

If I hire out my grocery shopping, I'll need to make and keep a master list of grocery items we frequently purchase, as well as what we need at that point in time. This new person wouldn't be walking through my house, trying to guess what type of peanut butter I like or knowing we're out of laundry detergent (yet). Once I have the list for them, they can get to the shopping. If I expect certain things a certain way, I would note that at this point.

The key is to overexaggerate the breakdown of what it will take to complete a task so you can teach it to someone else.

With that said, you also will need to know what you want, how you want it done, and when you want it done. Document each step you take when completing a task. Think small and exaggerated steps, almost like you're teaching a ten-year-old. Later on, you can eliminate obvious steps.

Here's an example with laundry:

1. Separate linens and towels from clothing.
2. Sort darks, lights, and whites into three piles.
3. Separate delicate items like underwear, bras, chiffon, and silk.
4. Start with dark clothing and examine for stains. Treat stains according to chart (provide chart).
5. Add detergent to washer.
6. Add clothing.
7. Close lid.
8. Select normal, then cold wash.
9. Press start.

You get the idea.

Even though pretty much everyone has done laundry at least once, not everyone does laundry the same way. The more detailed you are with your steps, the easier the training will be. This eliminates the need for tons of questions during the training process.

If a ten-year-old could read and follow your directions, you're on the right track.

Important note: even if you never outsource these tasks, it's important to have these types of documents or videos available in case of an emergency. If you're ever unable to serve your business (think car accident or long illness), someone can easily read or watch your training materials and keep your business running while you are away.

Step Small 3: Create an exaggerated step-by-step process of the task you want to hire out. Be as detailed as possible. (If you start with something like babysitting, create a list of expectations, favorite songs, tv shows, books, ICE numbers, etc., to help them make an easy transition.)

2. CREATE A JOB DESCRIPTION

Once you've created your training materials, the next step is to create a job description.

Start with an IAPW employee in mind. Ideally, what would you want from them? What types of personalities are easiest for you to work with? What qualities and experience would they have?

From here you need to craft a clear and concise job description. Here are the main components of a job description:

- Title - Your title should clearly capture the job objective.
- Type of Position - Full-time, part-time, project-based.
- Expected Tasks - Be specific, but don't belabor the details. That will come once you hire.
- Hours - How many hours do you plan to provide for them? Are they flexible or fixed?
- Payment - What are you willing to pay? For part-time, it's customary to provide an hourly wage and the maximum number of weekly hours ($10/hr with a 20-hour max). For projects, state the amount you'll pay for a specific project and your completion expectations. Method and frequency of payment should also be discussed.

Remember, your job description is the first impression potential applicants receive from you. When you review your job description, ask yourself: "Would I want to work for me based on this description?"

Sample Job Description

Personal Assistant for a busy home-based business owner.

I'm a very busy mom and business owner seeking help with many different tasks throughout my week. I am looking for an energetic, positive person to assist me with a multitude of domestic and personal tasks. This will be a part-time position starting at 10 hours a week split between two to three days. There is potential for increasing hours in the near future. The pay rate will be $12/hr, paid by check or direct transfer app every Friday.

Tasks include, but not limited to:

- Running errands such as grocery shopping, prescription pick-up, car wash, etc.
- Household calendar management.
- Light cleaning duties such as sweeping, folding laundry, vacuuming.
- Light food prep/cooking.
- Organizing and filing papers.
- Making and managing appointments.
- Booking travel arrangements.
- Managing pet care, children's play dates, and school events.

Now it's your turn.

Step Small 4: Write a job description for the task you want to hire out.

3. Find Help

Pat yourself on the back! That's a lot of work.

Now it's time to find the ideal person for the job. There are a few different ways to do this. You can visit employment websites, read through potential candidates who match your description, and reach out to them. Or you can post your job description, and wait for people to apply.

Where you post your job description or search for resumes will depend on what type of help you need. For someone to work in your home, start with your network of friends and family. If that doesn't work out, try Facebook marketplace, local churches, or moms' groups. For someone who will work remotely, Google can be your best friend.

Here are some suggested places to start looking for your candidate:

1. Word-of-mouth recommendations from trusted sources
2. Facebook marketplace
3. Local moms' groups
4. Church
5. Yelp reviews
6. Indeed.com
7. Angieslist.com for contractors
8. Upwork.com for virtual assistants, freelancers, online business managers, or support for larger projects
9. Care.com for babysitters, nannies, housekeepers
10. Fivver.com for small, inexpensive projects

If you want a business that brings freedom and enjoyment to your life, you'll have to lay aside the preconceived notion that you can (or should) do it all.

Step Small 5: Post your job description in one place, or search one site for a potential candidate.

Even if you could do it all, you can't do it all *well*. Ever heard the phrase, *Jack of all trades, master of none*? Maybe you can do it all—but how can you be *excellent* at anything when you're trying to do everything?

Megan, mama of two little ones and my longtime bestie, loves to catch some rays and blast her music while mowing the lawn. She calls it *Mommy's alone time*. For me, this is a despised task. I prefer cooking over lawn care any day! Believe it or not, there are people who love to clean, do laundry, and mow the lawn. Hire them to do what they love so you can do what you love.

Friends, you've got to stick to the most important things, like what you value most, what your deepest needs are, and what brings fulfillment and enjoyment.

Leave the rest to someone else!

STEP SMALLS IN THIS CHAPTER:

1. Make a list of small and big things (both domestic and business tasks) you can hire out. Get crazy here . . . think IAPW style.
2. You can hire out nearly anything. Whatever it is you need, narrow it down to one thing, and complete the following process before moving on to something else.
3. Create an exaggerated step-by-step process of the task you want to hire out.
4. Write a job description for the task you want to hire out.
5. Post your job description in one place, or search one site for a potential candidate.

Chapter 10

PLAN TO PIVOT

When life doesn't go as planned, you must learn to pivot.

Change can (and does!) happen monthly, weekly, or even daily. How you view and deal with change can determine the course of your life.

Handling change, and the disappointments that often come with them, is something we learn along the way. Though my husband and I decided we'd like to have kids one day, we didn't expect it to be as soon as it was! We didn't expect cars to break down in the middle of winter or money to be tight. Truth be told, we had no idea what to expect. That was part of the problem.

Let's be real. Adapting is difficult.

Most of the time change is forced upon us by an outside source. When I was pregnant with my third child, I developed gestational diabetes. My previous pregnancies were healthy and uneventful. Let's just say that this shock wasn't welcomed. All my plans for a natural, drug-free, midwife-guided birth changed in an instant. My doctor visits doubled, and I had to count kicks hourly. My baby's life was at risk. Learning to inject myself with insulin three times a day, and being immediately labeled as high-risk for complications, forced me to pivot.

Despite the inconvenience, I adapted to every change.

Some changes can be very positive—like getting married or having children. Even though we desire or expect the change, we still pivot in a new direction. The best way to do this (whether the change is positive or negative) is to expect that change will happen and often.

In other words: be ready for the unexpected.

"Expect the best. Plan for the worst. Capitalize on what comes."
—Zig Ziglar

Expecting the *best* is a mindset shift that success requires. You need to believe better things are possible before you start, or you'll self-sabotage your efforts with doubt.

Planning for the worst is a means of preparation. That's it. Don't hear what I'm not saying. I am *not* saying to sit around and anticipate doom and gloom. I certainly didn't plan to lose my home . . . but, we should have been a bit more prepared to handle financial hardship.

Prepare as if you'll obtain everything you work for. When our minds are ready to receive bigger things, we'll naturally see better opportunities.

Edna Mode

"Luck favors the prepared." —Edna Mode

Edna Mode is one of my all-time favorite characters.

Her role in *The Incredibles* movie is small, but powerful. Those of you who have seen it will remember her as the high-tech fashion designer for the superhero suits. She designs the entire family a set of supersuits according to their powers. Since she doesn't know the baby's powers, she builds in all kinds of features just in case.

When Mrs. Incredible is baffled by the multitude of features, Edna utters her famous phrase, "Luck favors the prepared."

She took precautions ahead of time. She paved the way for success.

While I love Edna, I also don't fully agree with her statement because I don't believe in luck. The word luck isn't doing it for me. Luck means success or failure is brought by chance rather than through one's own actions. I believe we *create* our own success based on our actions.

Instead, I would say, "*Opportunity* favors the prepared." Opportunity will present itself.

And, I will show you how to prepare.

The P.L.A.N. Blueprint

The P.L.A.N. blueprint stands for:

> P—Prepare
> L—Learn
> A—Apply
> N—Next step

As always, we are stepping small. This acronym will help you break down the overwhelm of making unexpected changes. It will teach you how to prepare your mind for change and take action even when it's hard. P.L.A.N is the next phase in the Dream Big IAPW groundwork you've been working on.

Prepare

"A goal without a plan is just a wish." —Antoine de Saint-Exupéry

Preparing for something you don't have yet seems a bit ridiculous.

Why spend time working on something that may never happen? The answer is simple. If you think, act, and prepare your schedule like a CEO, you'll become one.

We don't have to wait to arrive to start making adjustments to our lives. Think of it like the anticipation of going to an awesome party. We accept an invitation sent in advance and spend time planning for it. We buy a gift, pick our clothes, hire a babysitter, and more. The excitement continues to build as each step brings you closer to the main event. The *preparation* keeps your mind focused on how much fun you'll have. After all the preparation, you finally arrive and enjoy the amazing event.

Bottom line?

Start acting like the person you want to become. If your IAPW says you want to become a seven-figure business owner, you need to start preparing to become one. Anticipating what might come next and taking a step towards that will pay off. You don't become an expert or CEO because you were suddenly appointed. You earn it by taking action toward a goal. We prepare for a bigger role by being prepared for the unexpected.

The only thing we know for certain is change will come.

Part of being a business owner is developing the ability to pivot quickly. When I was first teaching online, long before Facebook Live, we used a platform called Spreecast, which was a live streaming platform you could broadcast from for a very small fee. Although clunky and unreliable, Spreecast was the perfect place for budding entrepreneurs to broadcast their live content for free.

Abruptly, Spreecast announced they were going out of business, and their users had thirty days to save their content, or it would be deleted forever. I panicked. Although subpar, I was comfortable with Spreecast! The thought of this sudden change made me cry. (Seriously. I cried. A lot. Technology is not my strong suit.)

I wasn't prepared for this. I didn't have another plan, so I had to change quickly if I still wanted to do live broadcasts. After the panic subsided, I had to scramble to find another platform, learn it, and change my whole system to make it work. It was the most stressful thirty days of my business.

I learned a very difficult lesson that day.

Having a backup plan is extremely important if your income depends on things you cannot control, like live broadcasting platforms, software, social media outlets, or similar things. Preparing for what may go wrong will set you up for success in the long run.

Let's be reminded that I am not asking you to constantly worry about doom and gloom. We're stepping small by thinking over what could go wrong in order to find possible solutions for major issues.

All too often, women believe we have to know how to do every-thing before we try it. We're often naturally more risk-averse and desire more information before we commit. This results in delayed action—it's a defense mechanism. Preparing helps avoid this be-cause we decide on a finish line, and then plan the next step. We don't need all four hundred steps to start. Just the very next step.

To prepare for the unexpected, we need to be aware of all the inner workings of our business. You need to know what the key pieces are that make your business run smoothly. In our case, a live streaming platform was our number one lead generator. The entire ship would sink if that went down.

Whatever those things are in your business, you'll need a list of them and possible alternatives. If, for example, Paypal is the major credit card payment processor you use to collect from your cli-ents, keep a list of alternative ideas in case they close their doors or change their policies.

There should be a master list of tasks—along with how often they're performed and by whom—as well as a list of programs, software, vendors, service providers, clients, account numbers, and contact information for each person in your business. This alone will help you avoid panic in the event of an emergency, or if a major part of your business changes in an unexpected way, even in a positive way.

Step Small 1: Prepare. If you haven't made your master business task list, now is the time. Make a list (or review the one you made) of all tasks performed in your business, software programs used, or service providers you rely on. If you aren't sure what's important, ask yourself this question, and fill in the name of the person, the service provider or software program. (Refer to the master task list you made in Chapter Nine when you were thinking about out-sourcing tasks.)

My business wouldn't work without _____.

(Paypal, YouTube, Facebook, Kajabi, Amazon, Hanlin Audio, Drip, etc.)

Step Small 2: List possible alternatives to major business tools.

- Paypal: Stripe, Square, Venmo
- YouTube: personal website, Twitch, Vimeo
- Facebook: be sure to collect emails from people to have a backup method of contact
- Kajabi: Teachable, Udemy, Thinkific
- Amazon: private website, eBay, Walmart seller site, Facebook marketplace, brick and mortar

Don't forget; we're not only anticipating change that could negatively impact our business, but we also need to plan for the changes needed as our business grows. As our businesses flourish, we'll outgrow our current tools and need to upgrade.

This is where we need to be prepared to *learn* new things.

LEARN

"The capacity to learn is a gift; The ability to learn is a skill; The willingness to learn is a choice." —Brian Herbert

You've prepared for your upcoming journey. You know where you'd like to end and where things could go wrong.

Now it's time to learn more.

Continuing to learn is essential for growth. To arrive at the top, you must strengthen your muscles for the climb. There is no elevator, no shortcut. You must take each step, learn what it takes to make the next move, and then make it.

This means learning new things. Notice how I didn't say *mastering* new things. Each leg of the race will require us to do more, learn more, and become more. We will have to learn new technology (Lord help me!), new skills, or deepen special character traits. When we dare to dream big, we accept the responsibility to arrive prepared!

The number one thing we can do to prepare is to learn.

Ways to Learn

Learning is not negotiable.

A lot of you are on your own with fixed budgets and limited time. I get it. Learning is necessary for growth, but it doesn't have to be expensive. Self-education allows us to learn in any format that works best for our situation, but without thousands of dollars in student loans.

There are only two rules to self-education:

1. Be consistent
2. Apply. (More on this soon.)

The 15-Minute Hustle is a great place to start (and makes it a lot easier to be consistent). There are countless ways to learn new things for free, and there is a perfect platform for everyone.

Here are just a few to get your mind going:

- **Visual:** For visual learners, YouTube is a wealth of information. Everything from growing indoor organic vegetables to how to train your hamster. (Yes, this is a thing.) If there a video tutorial exists, YouTube has it. Other inexpensive places to learn are video course sites like Udemy and Skillshare.
- **Audio:** For those who prefer listening to your education (and love multitasking!), podcasts are a great way to learn on-the-go. Podcasts span all topics and are one of the fastest growing forms of media. Listen while you work out, grocery shop, wash dishes, or drive. Audiobooks are another great way to learn.

- **Tactile:** Let's not underestimate good, old-fashioned books. Workbooks make me totally geek out. If reading is best for you, seek out books from leading experts.

- **Social:** One of the fastest ways to grow is face-to-face, one-on-one mentorship. The higher price tag is counterbalanced by how much it cuts off your learning curve. Speak directly with someone with specific expertise, who can educate you on the minutiae of your business.

Step Small 2: What is required of you in your dream job? Write down one skill you can learn right now to better prepare for that role. Be specific about how and where you will learn this new skill.

Example: In my dream job, I need to be an excellent verbal communicator. One skill I can learn right now is developing my signature talk. I can learn from the *Speaking Your Brand* podcast, blog, and perhaps a coaching session.

We cannot simply learn; we must apply our new knowledge to our lives. Learning is a wonderful step. Learning keeps our minds sharp and young.

However, learning is simply not enough by itself.

APPLY

"Knowing is not enough; we must apply. Willing is not enough; we must do."— Johann Wolfgang von Goethe

If learning doesn't bring change, it's useless.

If we simply learn and don't apply the new insights, we've wasted time and effort. When we learn something new, it's meant to change us. It leaves its mark and allows us to become a better version of ourselves.

Applying our newfound knowledge is one way we improve.

Application is putting into action what we've learned. We must practice our new skills and learn more as we experience trial and error. Make no mistake, practice will give us more experience, but it will never make us perfect.

As a recovering perfectionist, my business bestie Amy Feierman says it best, "Practice doesn't make you perfect; it simply makes you better." Don't expect to be perfect. Instead, aim to be better than you were yesterday.

Step Small 3: Apply what you've learned. What is one new thing you can apply in your business?

Example: I listened to the *Speaking Your Brand* podcast from Carol Cox. She suggests putting stories into your signature talk. To apply this new knowledge, I'll brainstorm stories from my life and other sources to include in my signature talk.

NEXT STEP

> *"You don't have to know everything about the mountain in front of you to take the next step." —Louie Giglio*

When you're comfortable with the first three phases of the P.L.A.N. Blueprint, it's time to move again.

The Next Step idea is the very foundation on which *Dream Big, Step Small* is built. It's a consistent, repeatable pattern. Steps are made to climb. Action is meant to be taken. When you've journeyed through preparing, learning, and applying, you move to the next step and repeat.

You don't have to master every task in your business. You simply need to learn enough to be comfortable with a new skill before you add more. Don't spend too much time trying to master everything.

We will always have a next step.

We will always have something to prepare for, something to learn, and something to apply. For some, learning is all about climbing higher. For others, it's a sideways step, a step away, or a step down. Whatever it is—there will be a step.

Next steps are part of life no matter who we are or what we're trying to accomplish. We'll walk through many seasons and stages of life—building, sustaining, even downsizing. Each stage will present different challenges, require new skills, and teach fresh truths to apply.

With the P.L.A.N. Blueprint, you'll always be armed to tackle your next step.

Whatever it may be.

Step Small 4: Now that you have prepared, learned, and applied your knowledge, what will your next step be? Add the collective small steps together, and create an overview that helps you decide your next step.

Example:

Prepare—I have created a list of alternative plans and tools to use if something in my business goes wrong or grows fast. My master task list is complete.

Learn—When I arrive at my dream job, I need to be an excellent verbal communicator. One skill I can learn right now is to develop my signature talk. I can learn from the *Speaking Your Brand* podcast and blog, and I will consider a coaching session.

Apply—I listened to a podcast from Carol, and she suggests putting stories into my signature talk.

Next—I will brainstorm stories from my own life experience and other sources that I can include in my signature talk. My Next Step is to outline and practice my signature talk.

Taking the next step is as easy as knowing *what* it is. When you know where you're going, it's easier to prepare. When you're prepared, it's easier to learn. When you learn, application is just around the corner.

Step Smalls in this Chapter:

1. Make a list (or review the one you made) of all tasks performed in your business, software programs used, or service providers you rely on.
2. What is required of you in your dream job? Write down one skill you can learn right now to better prepare you for that role.
3. Apply what you've learned. What is one new thing you can apply in your business?
4. Now that you have prepared, learned, and applied your knowledge, what will your next step be? Add the collective small steps together, and create an overview that helps you decide your next step.

Chapter 11

TRACK YOUR TIME

There are six books that have a permanent residence on my nightstand. I frequently refer to them for inspiration and a personal kick in the pants.

One of them is called *168 Hours: You Have More Time Than You Think,* by Laura Vanderkam. This book taught me the concept of time-tracking.

It changed my life.

MY BREAKTHROUGH

Coupled with my 15-Minute Hustle strategy, time-tracking is the holy grail of productivity. Until I started this strategy, I had no clue how distracted I became, or how much time I wasted. The idea that I, Kristin Ostrander, had the same 168 hours to spend each week as the President, Steve Jobs, or Oprah revolutionized the way I looked at my time. Before this, I felt like I used my time pretty well (in 15-minute chunks), but I realized that moments slipped away. Fast! My inner data nerd loved the concept of writing on paper everything I did. I couldn't wait to see the actual time stamps and what I accomplished.

At first, it was a bit like the Hawthorne Effect we talked about earlier. I was much more productive because I had to write my tasks down. It didn't take long, however, for me to get distracted.

I started by setting a 15-minute timer, then proceeded to tackle the first task on my list. That went extremely well. So, I reset the timer and began again. After three rounds, I forgot to reset the timer. Three hours later, I came back from the kitchen to find that I hadn't stuck to the plan. A phone call from a friend in the area had caught my attention. She asked me to go to lunch.

Hello? Yes, I wanted to go to lunch!

Any excuse to get out and be social is my thing—so much so that it sabotaged my productivity. This motivated me to look at other times I allowed myself to turn from my priorities, and then complain that I never had enough time!

Time-tracking changed everything.

Although I love going to lunch, I had to learn to say *no* or put it on the schedule. I value time with my friends (and impromptu lunches), but I also needed to get real about my business. Each time I said *yes* to a pop-up lunch break, I said *no* to the bigger picture.

HOLES IN THE BUCKET

The time-tracking proved that work required less time than I thought when I removed distractions and stayed focused.

I also discovered there were many holes in my bucket.

Time leaked out all over the place! Of course, I wanted to stop it. When I tracked every waking hour on paper, I could see how much time I spent on social media, Netflix, and with my kids. I could see where I sat in a parking lot, a waiting room, or a line at the store. Dinner didn't take that much time to make, actually. As the book title promised, I had more time than I thought. The experience humbled and excited me at the same time. I wasted a lot of time doing unimportant things, but I was eager to identify the time-wasters and reduce, or eliminate, them.

Immediate revolution.

How often have we left a room to do something, saw a sock on the floor, picked it up, headed to the laundry room to put it in the pile, then started a load of laundry, folded another load, and then, after thirty minutes, you couldn't remember why you got up to begin with?

Thanks to time-tracking, I easily found the holes in my bucket and plugged them with more productive—and most importantly, more fulfilling—things.

How to Time-Track

Step Small 1: Spend one day tracking everything you do in 15- to 30-minute increments.

Time-tracking is a simple exercise that can reveal all the holes in your bucket. Once you know where the leaks are, you can plug them with more important things. All you need is a comfortable way to track your activities. A timer isn't necessary, but extremely helpful, as a reminder. You could also use a note-taking app like Evernote or Colornote or a piece of paper.

It's as simple as a timestamp and an activity.

Mine would look something like this:

> *7:00-7:15: shower*
> *7:15-7:30: hair, makeup, dressed*
> *7:30-8:00: get Allie ready for school, make breakfast, pack lunch*
> *8:00-8:15: pack backpack, go to bus stop*
> *8:15-8:30: wait for bus*

You can be more detailed if you feel it will help. With business tasks, I recommend being extremely detailed. If you write *checking email,* that could be deceiving. We can get lost in our inbox with emails that aren't a priority.

Here is an example of how I track business tasks:

> *9:00-9:15: answer course questions*
> *9:15-9:30: Facebook group questions*
> *9:30-9:45: answer customer service emails*
> *9:45-10:00: check amazon orders*
> *10:00-10:30: research new catalog pages 84-86*

I use the Google timer on my chrome browser in the background or the timer on my phone. I set it for 15 minutes and get to work. When it goes off, I write down what I had been doing for the last 15 minutes and reset the timer.

If by chance you get off track during the 15 minutes, the timer will snap you back to reality. Remember—this is only for a few days. You don't have to live and die by the timer forever, but it greatly reduces rabbit trails and distractions. If short timers stress you out, adjust it. Thirty minutes or less is the recommendation. Any longer and we start to forget the exact tasks we completed and how long they took.

Once you've completed the time-tracking period, it's time to evaluate where all of your time is going.

This will be fairly eye-opening.

If you are honest, you'll see places in your day where you have more time than you think to sneak in a few extra tasks. I used to say that I loved reading but never had time to read. When I tracked my time, I realized I had at least thirty minutes in my day where I'd play a game on my phone. I'm not saying that playing games should be struck from the day—I consider it downtime for my brain. However, I love reading far more than games. Once I saw this on my time tracker, I asked myself: *what is more important to me, reading or playing games?* I chose reading. I decided to leave books in places throughout the house so I would see them more often and be reminded to read.

Additionally, I invested in Audible so I could listen to books while doing other things. I kept my favorite game on my phone and deleted the rest. I still play it, but now I have a way to reincorporate reading instead of making excuses.

We all have the same amount of time, so we need to make room for the most important things. If it has value to you, you'll make space for it. Time-tracking is a way to find more time for the things that are *most* important.

But how do you know what's most important?

Let's figure that out together.

What is Most Important?

Go back and revisit your IAPW. What does your day look like? What activities does it include?

If you're seeing things on your time-tracker that aren't in line with your IAPW, start there. Nowhere does my IAPW say to play games on my phone. That is a distraction keeping me away from what I really want. Reading, however, will always be part of my IAPW.

Make priorities based on what is most important. If you want to earn more income, you'll need to prioritize money-making tasks over leisure time. I love leisure time, and I think we should all have downtime in our lives, but we all have small changes we can make to enjoy leisure time but also make time for business-building. Remember one thing: one step is all you need to continue moving in the right direction.

Step Small 2: Comb over your time-tracker, and decide on one thing you will eliminate or reduce.

Before we close this chapter, I must be honest. I had never tracked my time before taking this challenge, but I had *kept time*.

Let me explain.

There is a cute tin sign in my office that says, *Don't rush me. I'm waiting until the last minute.*

This describes me perfectly. My husband, kids, and business bestie Amy will testify to this. For most of them, it's their least favorite thing about me.

My special way of *keeping time* has annoyed everyone I love many times. I track how long it takes me to do things and go places. I know exactly how long it takes me to shower, do my hair, makeup, and get dressed. It takes me exactly eight minutes to get to my sister's house, ten minutes for my daughter to find and put on her shoes, and one minute to the bus stop.

Maybe you don't play beat the clock. Perhaps you're always late because you have no idea how long it takes to complete a task. Maybe you're always fifteen minutes early for everything. No matter where you fall, the concept of time-tracking will open your eyes.

It reveals just how much time drains out of our lives and into the black hole of unimportance.

STEP SMALLS IN THIS CHAPTER:

1. Spend one day tracking everything you do in 15- to 30-minute increments.
2. Comb over your time-tracker, and decide on one thing you will eliminate or reduce.

Chapter 12

GET REAL ABOUT MONEY

Remember the business identity crisis I had when I went into cake decorating?

After pivoting back to my original love, eBay, I wanted to educate myself, act like a business owner, and take it seriously. I knew if I wanted to do something different, I needed to learn something new.

With a renewed sense of purpose, I set my mind to explore different ways to make my business more profitable.

As the search began, I discovered a wealth of educational resources I hadn't heard of before. Books to read, forums to join, newsletters to sign up for, and classes to take. I found an amazing book to teach me new sales strategies, improved eBay listings, and how to specialize in a niche.

The problem: these classes and books cost money.

One book I wanted was $50. It may not seem like much, but $50 was the difference between gas in the tank or walking. I hadn't been selling after the cake decorating detour. Because I wasn't selling, there wasn't any extra money to buy this book.

My current inspirational bubble burst.

That dreaded, haunting phrase kept creeping in . . .

"We can't afford it."

WE CAN'T AFFORD THAT

Let me tell you how much I despise this phrase.

This limiting phrase compares me to all the other people who *can* buy things that I *can't*. The sheer utterance of it reminds me of all the times I wanted something in my childhood but couldn't have it.

Growing up in a single parent family meant there wasn't a lot of money. At my friend's house, snacks filled the cupboards. All the good cereal, all the best cookies, snack crackers, and pop. (Yes, I am from the midwest. We say pop here instead of soda.) In our house, we had plenty to eat, but not those things because they were *expensive*. While at the grocery store with my dad, I'd ask for brand name cereal, pop, and cookies.

He'd always say, "We can't afford that."

I remember a specific trip to the store when I wanted a box of cereal that came with a special book, stickers, and activities inside. I asked my Dad as he perused the cheaper options, "Can we get this instead?"

"That kind is too expensive, and we can't afford it," he said.

With a sassy little foot stomp, I said, "When I grow up, I'm going to buy whatever cereal I want!"

At eight years old, I didn't have a clue what money was, how to get it, or even how to *keep* it, but I knew that saying, "We can't afford it," limited my choices.

Please don't hear what I'm not saying.

I'm not saying my dad should have bought expensive things because I wanted them. What I am saying is that words have a lasting impact, especially when attached to money. What we're taught about money at a young age can make a difference in our adult lives. It makes a difference in how we think about it, relate to it, obtain it, and spend it.

What we believe about money will affect everything in our lives, especially in business.

Limiting Money Scripts

As I sat staring at the computer screen, wanting to buy that $50 book I couldn't afford, all the negative dialogue came flooding back.

The same old scripts played through my head:

"You should've stayed in college to get a good job. Then, you wouldn't be in this position."

"Dad was right. If I'd stayed in school, I would probably be making big money right now."

"You'll never be able to afford the good stuff."

"You will always barely get by."

I clicked off the computer screen as tears welled up in my eyes, defeated. I couldn't afford the $50 book. Everything felt hopeless.

But it wasn't.

We're going to talk about ways you can stop yourself from falling into that hole (and teach your kids, right now, to have a positive money mindset.)

Let's go.

LIMITING MONEY BELIEFS

We have all uttered that dreadful, "We can't afford it," phrase. To ourselves, our spouses, our kids. There are many other beliefs we have about money and how we relate to it that affect the decisions we make.

How about these other ones?

- I'll never be able to retire.
- Debt is a part of life; we will always have it.
- Vacations are for rich people.
- Wealthy people are greedy.
- More money, more problems.
- I'll always live paycheck-to-paycheck.
- I can't save money.
- I don't have a degree; I can't earn more.
- Less is more.
- You get what you pay for.

- Be happy with what you've got.
- Money won't make you happy.
- I'm broke.

If you find yourself saying these things, you're not alone.

We have all said them. Some of us say them on a regular basis. From a young age, our parents and other influences have taught us our beliefs about money—how we earn it, save it, and spend it.

No matter where you came from or how you were raised, I believe whoever brought you up did the best they could. They taught you what they thought was right. No matter what happened, you developed a belief system about money by tuning into the people around you and how they related to money.

FLIPPING THE SCRIPT

The same old script you have played over and over doesn't have to remain there. You can swap it for a healthier version and begin owning new truths.

One of the greatest things about being an adult is the ability to make choices. As a child, we're inundated with other people's thoughts, ideas, and preferences. When we're grown, we have more freedom to choose different ideals than our parents. Guess what?

That is perfectly ok.

You're a unique individual. You're living in a different generation with new technologies and new perspectives. This is your permission to do life your way. Try on a new script instead of the old one that is no longer serving you in a positive way.

Here are some common money scripts and new thoughts to try on instead.

Old Script: I'm broke.
New Script: I am a hard worker, and I am capable of improving my income.

Old Script: I'll never be able to retire.
New Script: I can take small, consistent steps to plan for my future.

Old Script: Debt is a part of life; we will always have it.
New Script: Debt is a choice. As my income increases, I can choose to live differently.

Old Script: Vacations are for rich people.
New Script: I am worthy of a vacation regardless of my income. I can plan for it.

Old Script: Wealthy people are greedy.
New Script: Wealthy people have worked extremely hard and are wise with their money. I can learn to do the same.

Old Script: More money, more problems.
New Script: More money gives me more options to help more people. It is a tool, neither good nor bad.

Old Script: I'll always live paycheck-to-paycheck.
New Script: Money is abundant. I can learn new skills to earn more money.

Old Script: I can't afford to save money.
New Script: I can save pocket change in a jar as a small step.

Old Script: I don't have a degree; I can't earn more.
New Script: I am smart. I can learn new marketable skills to increase my income.

Old Script: Less is more.
New Script: I can choose to spend my resources in any way that feels right for me. I am worthy of taking care of myself in a way that feels good for me and my family.

Whether you relate to all of these (or very few), everyone's relationship with money could use improvement. Some women may feel like they're betraying their past, their parents, or their upbringing by abandoning these thoughts. This isn't what you are doing. You are aligning your choices with your IAPW by stepping closer to a better version of yourself. There is no shame in that, only hope for a better future that you're choosing to create.

Step Small 1: Flip your script. Chose three limiting money beliefs you've believed, and practice replacing the old phrase with the new phrase.

INTERNALIZING OTHERS' BELIEFS

My father was a simple man.

He came from simple means and was always thankful and satisfied with the small things. Family. His job. Good health. He never wanted or needed much. When I was young, there was a show on TV called *Lifestyles of the Rich and Famous*. Long before Instagram and Facebook showed ordinary people with mega mansions, this show gave the average American a sneak peek into the lives of celebrities and the ultra-rich.

Everything was huge. Mansions, yachts, rooftop pools. Luxury abounded, including fancy cars, diamond chandeliers, and private tropical islands. The show fascinated me. My dad, on the other hand, wasn't as thrilled.

"You could feed a whole country for a year with what that house cost. What a waste of money," he said one night as he flipped through the channels.

I'm certain he wasn't trying to teach me a limiting belief about money; he was just giving his opinion. What I internalized on that day, however, was that having a lot of money was bad. If you had a lot of money, you should feed small countries. Having nice things (and enjoying them) was selfish.

Did he actually say those exact things?

No.

Somewhere inside his comment, however, a young, impressionable pre-teen developed this belief. I grew up feeling guilty for wanting more. I had to justify any purchase or upgrade. Shame overwhelmed me if I wanted to purchase a new car, an extra pair of shoes, or go on a vacation. I never wanted to be labeled as greedy or ungrateful.

One of the breakthrough moments I had about my limiting money beliefs was hearing Dave Ramsey say on one of his radio programs, "Money isn't good or bad. It's just a tool."

This changed my thinking.

I could relate to tools.

My dad was a woodworker and a handyman, so tools were always around. When I pictured a hammer or a drill, I didn't have any positive or negative feelings about them. They were neither good nor bad. The tool analogy was the *ah-ha* moment that changed my entire perspective. Tools were used for a purpose and helped you fix and build things.

With money as a tool, I could now remove the emotional attachment and rephrase these thoughts into something new. Instead of thinking having a lot of money is greedy, I could use my higher income to fix and build. I can fix things! I help people in need, build my retirement account, and save for my children's education.

This thought was liberating.

MONEY FREEDOM

So why all this money talk? I'll cut right to the chase.

We all carry limiting beliefs around with us.

Many of these beliefs are buried deep and haven't seen the light of day in decades. If we don't dig them up, deal with them, and create new beliefs, we'll never give ourselves the freedom to achieve our IAPW.

These beliefs sabotage our success. If we believe something is bad, we avoid it. If we believe we're not worthy of something, we'll subconsciously stop ourselves before we get too close.

Listen, friends; God has given you a unique set of skills, talents, and gifts. If you have a passion for something, God has given that to you. It isn't wrong to earn money while using your God-given gifts. In fact, He promises to equip you with all that you need to carry out that passion and purpose (Hebrews 13:21).

That includes money.

1 Timothy 5:18 says, "The laborer is worthy of their wages." God has declared you worthy of your wage.

Friends, earning your wage isn't bad or greedy. It's a direct reward for your efforts. A *worthy* reward.

Here's the important part—this is where you get to decide what to believe about money from now on. You no longer have to hold on to past beliefs. As a grown adult, you can decide to agree or disagree with the beliefs that were directly or indirectly bestowed upon you.

Do you still agree with the things you were taught?

Do you have new ideas and thoughts about money that you'd like to embrace?

Think about the circumstances in your life that could change if you related to money differently. You hold the key to your own thoughts and belief system. When you learn something new, you can open the door to a new thought process. Or you can stay locked inside the cell of old beliefs.

Once you have the key (which I've just given you! Let's flip the script!), you have the ability to either unlock the door or stay inside.

Step Small 2: Write down circumstances or events that shaped or reshaped how you felt, thought, and related to money. Explore new ideas, thoughts, and concepts. (Use flip the script suggestions as your guide). Take the time to explore what has been holding you back. Try to recall concepts you learned about money throughout your life.

Step Smalls in this Chapter:

1. Flip your script. Chose three limiting money beliefs you've believed, and practice replacing the old phrase with the new phrase.
2. Write down circumstances or events that shaped or reshaped how you felt, thought, and related to money. Explore new ideas, thoughts, and concepts. (Use flip the script suggestions as your guide). Take the time to explore what has been holding you back. Try to recall concepts you learned about money throughout your life.

Chapter 13

THE UGLY CRY

Brace yourself; this could get ugly.

You are my friend, so I can be brutally honest with you, right? Great, because I've been doing that since the first word of this book, and I can't stop now! I care about you, your business, and your family.

That's why I want to give you a bit of a warning.

This journey you are on is going to be beautiful.

A beautiful *mess*.

Building your IAPW can be ugly at times. Very ugly. No one warned me about the hard parts.

I had this dream idea in my mind that someday I'd arrive at a sunshine and rainbows destination with long walks on the beach. If my income hit a certain level, I could sip margaritas brought by a pool attendant while the cash rolled in. I had never talked with anyone who had a seven-figure business, so I didn't know the reality. Wasn't there a magic number I could hit, and all my problems would disappear?

Not. Even. Close.

The truth is best summed up by Joyce Meyer, a Christian author and teacher who said, "New levels, new devils."

When you reach a new level in business, whether it's more revenue, more profit, or a growing team, your problems don't decrease—they change.

Have you ever thought this, *If I had more money, everything would be better?* I certainly have. Many times. Money would solve a lot of my problems, right? Truth be told, an increase in resources *has* changed things for us. Many of those changes have had a positive impact, but new, unanticipated problems have arisen too.

Part of this is because as your business and income grow, so do your responsibilities. A sobering Bible verse, Luke 12:48, says, "To whom much is given, much shall be required." Instead of a walk down easy street, the bigger your business grows, the harder the decisions become.

Don't get me wrong, with increased income there are many new benefits. But expect an increase in responsibility and pressure. More people will rely on you. As you hire people, their income relies on the success of your business. It's directly on you to make sure your business runs smoothly. It's a higher call to excellence.

The real pressure comes from other places, not just business. Life will challenge you. Loved ones will pass away. Children will get sick. Emergencies arise. You have to juggle multiple struggles in business and in your personal life.

This is where it gets ugly. This is where I get real with you.

No matter how many digits are in your bank account, you're going to have problems. If you have relationship issues with your mother-in-law right now, they won't disappear. If your child has special needs, that won't change. Sickness, loss, and unexpected events happen whether we have an enviable zip code or not.

When you have the responsibility of running a business *and* taking care of unexpected life issues, you need the right skills to handle it. The stress, the pressure, the emotions, and the ability to get back up from any setback.

I'm sorry this is heavy. I want to pave the way for you with realistic expectations. Please don't run away from your dreams. Sunshine and rainbows will come; just anticipate a few earthquakes, rainstorms, quicksand traps, and hurricanes too.

ENTER THE UGLY CRY

Just a few years ago, we had a healthy income, two thriving businesses, and a happy family. Life was better than it had ever been.

Then, the sick year happened.

After my husband's first injury and surgery when we had nothing to lean on, we learned our lesson the hard way. Accidents and illness can bring you to financial ruin. This time, we had decent savings, insurance, and an emergency fund. What we didn't know was what *this* kind of year could do to a family financially, spiritually, and emotionally.

Four surgeries in twelve months, long hospital stays, a new lifelong diagnosis, and endless doctor visits hit us that year. We had to change diets, deal with digestive issues, and the unexpected loss of two loved ones.

Along with all that came all the associated, unexpected, uncovered costs.

I felt like I was drowning. The heartache and tension from dealing with death, health issues, and the weight of the financial burden was more than I could bear. Relationships became tense. Finances tightened. Our savings account hit negative digits. The busiest season of my business crept closer. How could I small step my way through this kind of mounting pressure?

When would relief come?

Stepping small was the only way to manage the stress.

We cut back on our lifestyle to cover medical expenses. We had conversations to ease the grief and established new boundaries while sharing the same space. After a month of accepting our new normal, we began to inch closer to where we were before the hurricane of issues flooded our life.

But that didn't take care of a mounting problem: me.

I wasn't sleeping. I wasn't caring for myself. Resentment, anger, and an emotional breakdown fast approached. I couldn't handle one more thing. Hope was on the horizon though. Our anniversary trip was coming up. This gave me something to look forward to while working through our crazy mess. It would be a chance to breathe and escape for a short time. I could make it through anything if I knew that trip was almost here.

Then, an unexpected stomachache quickly turned from an ER visit, to an overnight stay, and then, surgery for my son—right before we were about to go on our trip. I walked out of my son's hospital room, down the hall to a bench . . .

. . . and completely lost it.

Right then and there, I cried.

Not just any cry, the *ugly* cry. The mascara-down-your-face-can't-breathe-through-the-snot kind of cry. I couldn't handle one more defeat. The entire universe stood in my way. Just when I thought we were on the road to recovery, another wave knocked us down. Every time I climbed over a wall, I had to face a taller one. There was no way I could turn around and do it again. My sore muscles hadn't recovered from the last fight.

Why Is the Ugly Cry Important?

After the ugly cry, I wanted to quit. I wanted to give it all up. How could I try and be a good mom, wife, and business owner when all these issues kept coming at us?

Worry, fear, and doubt flooded my mind. But whether we faced family emergencies or business failures, we need to address the issues and work through them. The truth is, they happen to all of us. Life doesn't discriminate. Whether we run a business or not these things happen to everyone in some form or another. We've got to learn to deal with the issues.

How?

We need to *do* the ugly cry. To admit we don't have it all togeth-er. We're all a beautiful, hot mess.

And that's okay.

No one has it all together. So, get the tissues, and cry it out. Talk to God; yell at the sky. Do what you've got to do. I fall apart frequently, and I'm still here. (I didn't die though ;)

Through the curveballs, we develop the ability to handle what comes our way. Our inner thoughts and emotions are at the center of our decision-making. Whether it's a costly business mistake or a death in the family, unexpected trouble finds us. Internal turmoil and negative thoughts will try to destroy us.

Do any of these sound familiar?

1. Why does this keep happening to me?
2. If all these things keep standing in my way . . . maybe I'm on the wrong path?
3. I'm taking time away from my kids to pursue business, and now I am failing at both.
4. What will people think if I do all these things and fall on my face?
5. What if I never get past the hurdles?
6. I'm so embarrassed that I didn't know about all this busi-ness stuff.
7. I'm working so hard, and my growth is so slow; I'll never make it anywhere.
8. All these setbacks ruined my progress; I'll never recover.

Friends, the struggle is real.

We allow these things to swarm around inside our heads. The frustration and emotions are real. That's why acknowledging and embracing *why* you feel what you feel is so important. The good news is when you acknowledge how you feel, and explore *why* you feel this way, you can begin to make changes.

Name It and Claim It

There are many ways to acknowledge and explore crippling self-doubt and the emotions that follow. When I'm feeling these self-defeating emotions, I do many things. I cry it out, pray through it, write it all down, or verbalize it to someone else.

Ways to Acknowledge Your Feelings

1. Express them verbally to a trusted friend.
2. Give yourself permission for a set period of time to feel any way you want.
3. Pray about it.
4. Write a letter to yourself expressing exactly what you feel even if it is really bad.
5. Say it out loud.
6. Scream it.
7. Cry it.

Write it, speak it, or even ugly cry it. Don't hold it back. No one sees this but you. It can be very freeing when we give acknowledgment to what we feel—even if it seems ridiculous. We tend to over-think emotions and dismiss them as silly or unimportant. Even though no one else might know what we are feeling, we often feel ashamed within ourselves for feeling the way we feel.

Acknowledging your feelings will help you validate them. Instead of dismissing them as ridiculous or hoping they magically disappear, just *own* them. We are emotional beings. If you feel guilty, you feel guilty. Name it and claim it. Once you do that, you can explore the reason for it, and move on.

Let's revisit Mommy Guilt.

We often believe we're neglecting our children or missing their lives because we're working. That's a real thing. It's a constant push-pull we face as working moms. Especially if we work from home and juggle domestic duties, business projects, and family time. Guilt sets in when we feel we're neglecting one for the other. Acknowledging the way you feel is how you navigate this feeling.

When you write down what you feel, start with the "I feel" phrase.

It can look something like this:

I feel guilty. I feel bad for not going on the school field trip. I feel guilty that I have no desire to go. I feel guilty that my house is a mess. I feel like a horrible mom for not spending more time playing with my kids. I feel guilty that I don't want to play with Barbie dolls. I feel guilty when I work. I fear my kids think I love work more than I love them.

This is a brain dump of everything you feel. The ugly and irrational, anything and everything. I'll say this again—these are your inner thoughts and feelings. No one is looking or judging.

I often write all this out, then tear it into tiny pieces and throw it away. If you hate playing barbies with your kids, it's ok to acknowledge that. If you feel guilty for buying frozen dinners, write it out. That doesn't make you a horrible person.

It makes you normal, human and real.

Step Small 1: Acknowledge at least one thought or feeling that's affecting you right now. Have you ugly cried recently? Perhaps start there.

THE EXPLORATION PHASE

Next is the exploration phase. This is where we uncover why we feel what we feel. It can start with you writing down "I feel guilty because . . ." and then let your mind run. You have full permission to feel all the feels.

How to Explore Your Feelings

For me, this always starts with a pile of sharpies, a mug of hot coffee, and a brainstorming session. I empty my brain onto the paper. The good, the bad, the ugly. For you, it can be anything you want. Screaming into a phone, pretending someone is listening. A quiet notebook in bed. Sitting alone at Starbucks. Whatever it might look like for you, it's time to explore.

We already acknowledged *what* we are feeling, but now we need to dig deeper into *why* we feel this way. Is it pressure from society? Our mother-in-law? A belief system that we should be doing something differently? Are someone else's expectations weighing you down?

Negative emotions overwhelm me when I feel I'm falling short of what I assume others expect. I constantly feel guilt for not volunteering in my daughter's classroom. Guilt for not being productive haunts me when I take a break. I like playing with my kids, but I don't love dolls. When my daughter wants to play dolls, I either suffer through it for fifteen minutes, or I say *no*.

Then, the guilt follows.

As an example, here's a way I explored some of my Mommy Guilt on paper:

I feel guilty because I have time and flexibility to go on the school trip, but I don't want to. I feel like people are judging me for not volunteering at school. I feel guilty because I should participate more in my kids' school. I feel guilty for watching TV when I have work to do. I feel guilty because my kids ask me to play with them, but I hate playing with dolls, so I say no. I feel guilty because my kids ate a PB&J for dinner. I feel guilty that I like my work more than I like Candyland. I feel guilty because I fantasize about weekends away.

Once you feel you've dumped it out, take some time to read over it. It's important to recognize that many negative emotions stem from unmeasured and unmet expectations we *impose on ourselves.*

Here's that again: we impose unmeasured and unmet expectations on ourselves.

It starts with us imagining what people must be thinking as they observe our lives. Maybe it sounds like this in our heads:

- "The teacher must think I don't care about my child's education because I don't volunteer at the school."
- "I've been so busy working on my business that we've had take-out every night this week. I am such a bad mom for not cooking."
- "I told my daughter I couldn't play Barbies right now. She must feel unloved because I said no and didn't play with her."
- "I feel guilty for pursuing a higher level of success in my business because I'm fearful it makes me look greedy or self-centered. Everyone will think I am money hungry and ungrateful for what I already have."

Step Small 2: Explore the reasons you feel whatever emotions are in your mind right now. Explain one of your emotions by writing it on paper. Concentrate on *why* you feel this way. Keep different scenarios in mind as you explore the reason. (Pressure from friends or family to do something; society says to do it; your upbringing told you it was the right thing, etc.) Start with "I feel _____ because _____."

Getting to the truth and separating the facts from the feelings will help us deal with the emotions that instantly halt our progress.

Reconcile

The final step is to reconcile the truth with what we've felt. This is where we practice trusting the facts about a situation instead of how we feel.

Let's revisit my lack of volunteerism at my daughter's school. After not volunteering to go on a trip with her class, I felt Mommy Guilt. My daughter felt sad, and I felt like I let her down. Guilt for not creating time in my schedule haunted me. Obligation crept in after it. Was I a bad mom for prioritizing work over a field trip?

These were the feelings.

The real facts were much different.

The feelings came from self-imposed standards and assumptions of what others might be thinking or feeling about my choices.

Here are some real facts about the situation:

- Many parents cannot attend field trips for many reasons.
- Earning income and providing for my children is important.
- There will be other times to participate in field trips.
- I am not obligated.
- I don't have to say yes just because I am asked.
- I am in control of what lands on my schedule.
- There are many ways to contribute to the school without going on field trips.
- I spend time with my children in other ways.
- It is ok to not enjoy school field trips.
- My daughter still feels loved even though I didn't go.

Now that I had acknowledged my feelings, explored why I was feeling them, and wrote down the facts, I was able to list possible resolutions for the gap between truth and feeling. Based on the facts, I can reframe the circumstance and speak a new truth to myself:

"I can't assume others are judging me. Even if they are, that's their problem. I can let go of fearing what they might think. I won't change my life to please others and avoid judgment."

"My children love me. I show them love, and I am actively involved in their lives daily. I don't need to go on field trips for them to feel loved."

"I contribute to the school in other ways. I don't need to feel bad for not doing everything."

Acknowledging, exploring, and reconciling will take practice. When the negative feelings creep up again, and they will, start the process over again. Over time, this gets easier. It won't go away. We'll always have negative feelings, but with each attempt to change them, we arrive at a happier place a lot faster.

Step Small 3: Write the true facts about the situation causing you negative emotions. Reconcile them with how you have been thinking and feeling, and write a new phrase you can choose to think about when the negative emotions attack.

So why all this emotional stuff in a business book?

Friends, we are emotional creatures.

Emotions affect all our decisions, including the ones about our business. Remember, we make decisions based on how we feel about a situation. If we're fearful, we'll make choices based on fear. That will hold us back.

If we feel guilty, we'll prioritize tasks we think we *should* do. Then, our business will be put on the back burner yet again.

We will always have emotions, whether they are good or bad. But this chapter gives you permission to *feel* all the feels no matter what. Go ahead and do the ugly cry. It will help! You're allowed to sit on the curb and cry, but it's not your permanent home. Just a place to rest while you pull yourself together.

The Step Smalls in this chapter are your roadmap back to the path of your IAPW. These steps will help you deal with those nasty emotions in a healthy and productive way so you can move toward your big dreams.

Step Smalls in this Chapter:

1. Acknowledge at least one thought or feeling that's affecting you right now. Have you ugly cried recently? Perhaps start there.
2. Explore the reasons you feel whatever emotions are in your mind right now. Explain one of your emotions by writing it on paper. Concentrate on *why* you feel this way.
3. Write the true facts about the situation causing you negative emotions. Reconcile them with how you have been thinking and feeling, and write a new phrase you can choose to think about when the negative emotions attack.

Chapter 14

ENJOY THE JOURNEY

Before we close out this journey, there's one more important aspect about stepping small: enjoying the journey.

I know, I know. It's easier said than done.

When our home foreclosed, we were looking at a negative bank account and a home ripped from our fingers. Joy was the last emotion in my heart.

But then, I got tired of feeling defeated.

I needed a way to feel successful immediately. Taking one small step helped me move in a positive direction.

But, adding gratitude to the small step changed *everything*.

When all Hell is breaking loose, gratitude is a pillar of strength. A way to feel good that doesn't cost you anything. It shifts our mindset to a positive place, instead of swirling in fear and doubt.

There's always something to be grateful for, even when everything seems to be falling apart. By practicing gratitude, you can find joy in the simple things and learn to enjoy each step. If you embrace the journey, the destination—or how long it takes to get there—won't matter as much. If you're enjoying the experience, the journey will be as rewarding as the arrival.

Let me tell you a little secret: there is no arrival.

Take it all in. Enjoy each step. Want to earn a million dollars? Sure. You'll get there. But enjoy your first six-figure year. Your first five-figure month. Celebrate each small step. Because if you wait until you "arrive" at a destination to find joy, you're missing out on life.

Slow Down

Our entire lives are a series of beginnings and ends, changes and adjustments.

The older I get, the more I realize how fast the time goes. If we're always rushing to the next place, we're missing what is here and now. Slowing down and staying in the moment enables us to see that there's much to be learned and enjoyed. We're not in a race. You don't have to build the next thing today. Take time after finishing a big project to enjoy that journey. Think about how you feel after completing something. What was fun for you during this time? What made you feel like you were on top of the world?

Step Small 1: Start a gratitude journal. Write five things you're thankful for today.

Focus on the Present

Small steps feel slow.

They feel like we're so far away from where we want to be. This is where we need to shift our focus onto the present.

When it comes to the past and the future, we only need reminders. Think of peeking behind a curtain at your past to remember how far you've come. We're only peeking! Don't tear open the curtain and dwell on it or dissect it. We're not there anymore. We've moved through those things, good or bad, and learned from them.

It's the same for the future.

Our IAPW is a peek into the future. It gives us hope. It spurs us on. But again, it's only a peek. We don't want our focus behind a curtain we can't fully see. It will only distract us from what's happening right now.

Think of each small step as a brick.

One brick alone isn't much. If you're consistent in laying down bricks every single day, you'll build a foundation quickly. Now imagine three months from now. If you take a small step every day toward your IAPW, you'll have ninety bricks on your foundation.

Those ninety bricks look a lot bigger when you stack them together.

That is what small, consistent steps look like when added together. When you get discouraged by slow progress, look at the bricks you've already put in place. Progress is still progress, no matter how small it seems.

Don't buy into the idea that everyone is moving faster than you. Maybe they are—but most likely they aren't. What you see on social media isn't the full story. It's a highlight reel! What no one is showing you is that behind the scenes there are years of failures, restarts, pivots, and ugly cries.

Every business moves slower than you think, it just isn't talked about. Jeff Bezos started Amazon from his garage. All by himself. Now that he's a billionaire, no one talks about that. Instead, they mention how he is one of the smartest and richest men in the world. Oprah was fired as a reporter. She's now worth over three billion dollars.

No one starts at the top. We all start as beginners. Each of these people (and any other successful business owner you see) started slow. They took consistent steps toward a dream. They didn't give up when it was hard; they learned to work through disappointments and pivot. You've been armed with the right information to do the same

Right here, right now.

Step Small 2: Find the joy in each step you take. Document three things that bring you joy—right now—so it feels more real. After each small step you take in the future, record what you're thankful for or why it was enjoyable.

STEP SMALLS IN THIS CHAPTER:

1. Start a gratitude journal. Write five things you're thankful for today.
2. Find the joy in each step you take. Document three things that bring you joy—right now—so it feels more real.

ADDITIONAL STEP SMALLS

Are you ready for more Step Smalls?

I've got your back.

I love having a list and someone telling me what to do, so I've created some additional steps for you to take if you want to keep upleveling your business.

You ready?

Let's go.

CHAPTER 2—DESIGN YOUR IAPW

1. Write the IAPW for your workday. What tasks does it include? What tasks *doesn't* it include?
2. Write the IAPW for your dream vacation. Where would you go? What would you do? What kinds of foods would you eat? What would you *not* do on your perfect vacation?
3. Pick the one word you want to feel when you look at your calendar (or planner or scheduler). Now list three things you can do to work toward that word right now.
4. Pick one word that you want to feel when you look at your financials. Do you feel that now? List why you do, or do not, feel your word. Then, write down three small steps to work toward it.
5. With your ultimate business IAPW in mind, make a list of things that will get you closer to it. Break each item down into several actionable steps. Now take 1-2 of those small steps, and put them into your schedule over the next five days.

CHAPTER 3—SELF-DISCOVERY

1. Look at the options for job opportunities on your list, and write a pros and cons list for each. What did you learn about each option?
2. Take your list to a trusted friend or partner, and ask them what they think. What qualities do they see in you that would inform job opportunities for you?
3. Make your own *Things I'd Love to Get Paid For* list. What falls on there? Choose your top three.
4. Write down your biggest fears about trying another career. Why are you afraid of those specific things? Is there a history behind them?

CHAPTER 4—TRUST THE FACTS, NOT THE FEELINGS

1. Have you had any *pinch me* moments? Make a list of all the ones you can remember, and describe *why* they were so important.
2. Write a list of fears in your life that may be holding you back in your business. (For example, you may write: *I'm afraid my mother-in-law will judge me for wanting to see sexy clothes, so I haven't started my lingerie business.*)
3. Have you ever failed? Why did you fail? List a few examples; look back over the list; and forgive yourself for them. Resolve to move on.
4. Dig a little deeper on your limiting beliefs. Identify a memory of a time when you didn't take action because of a limiting belief. Now identify how it impacts you today. Could you be doing that again without realizing? How could your life be different without that? Now let it go; forgive yourself; and move on.

CHAPTER 5—OWN YOUR OWNERSHIP

1. Think of four other business owners that you admire. How do they present themselves? What can you learn from how they speak about their business?
2. Practice introducing yourself as the CEO in front of a mirror. I'm serious. How does it feel?
3. Go to the store and buy a power outfit. That's an outfit that, every time you wear it, makes you *feel* like the CEO you are. It should be empowering.

CHAPTER 6—THE 15-MINUTE HUSTLE

1. Write down a list of ten things that you could 15-Minute Hustle your way through successfully. Can you do two of those today?
2. Plan out three 15-Minute Hustle activities to do with your children, and then do one each day. Be sure to reflect on how it felt.
3. Find one other working mom and ask them what they experience Mommy Guilt over. Is it similar to yours?

CHAPTER 7—FAKE IT 'TIL YOU MAKE IT

1. Make a list of twenty things that feel like self-care, and put it somewhere you'll see it every day—to keep this top of mind. (I provided a list in the chapter, but don't just steal off that. Make this specific to you.)
2. Write down why you're doing what you're doing. Why did you start this business? What is your IAPW around it?
3. Find a visual representation of your business IAPW, and

slap it on your mirror to look at every day. When you don't feel like faking it, take a look at that picture.

4. Plan out a big self-care event. (Tropical vacation. Trip to Vegas. Two nights in a hotel room without kids.) What small steps would you need to take to make it happen? If you can plan it, do it. Knowing that you move closer to that every day can be very motivational.

Chapter 8—Accountability is Everything

1. Make a list of things you've been meaning to get done, but haven't yet. Prioritize the top three as most important, and then talk to your accountability partner about it.

2. Feeling paralyzed or scared by these steps? Use the steps from Chapter 4, *Trust the Facts, Not the Feelings*, to figure out why.

3. Part of finding a good accountability partner is being one yourself. Write down five ways you could leverage your strengths to help someone else achieve their goals.

4. Communication is essential. Decide that way you want to be accountable to someone else. (Texting? Emails? Skype dates?)

Chapter 9—Getting Help

1. The idea of documenting all the processes of your business is overwhelming, so let's start smaller. Feel free to do each of these tasks at separate times, or all at once. Whatever feels best.

2. Choose a notebook, or create a document on your computer, and title it *Job Descriptions*.

3. Don't jump right into the descriptions yet if it feels like too much. Just make your list of tasks here.

4. Pick one task that appeals to you, and write each step down with bullet points; don't worry about details yet.

5. Go back, and fill in the details.

6. Read through it one more time? Feel alright? Now do it with another task.

7. Design your IAPW for hiring help. How would the process look? Visualize your perfect hire—right down to the everyday tasks that bring *them* joy.

8. Even if you don't have any jobs or projects to hire out yet, design an IAPW for project management anyway. Get your mind on growing into that place so you're ready when it comes.

Chapter 10—Plan to Pivot

1. Look at your business and decide the top three things you need to plan for. Is it growth? A new hire? Can you prepare for a possible event that would remove you from the business for a short time?

2. List ways you've already had to pivot in your business. What came of them? What did you learn?

3. List five big opportunities for your business that you can begin to plan for. Creating a path makes our success inevitable.

Chapter 11—Track Your Time

1. What do you say *yes* to at the expense of your bigger picture goals? Write down five things that sabotage your time. Then, write one Step Small to stop that from happening.

2. Separate money-making tasks from general business tasks

(such as checking email—unless that email generates money.) How can you prioritize money-making tasks better?

3. Let's dive into a deeper analysis of how you've used your time. What leisure activities were you using? How long on email? Product creation? Lead generation? Making dinner? What was most surprising about this exercise?

CHAPTER 12–GET REAL ABOUT MONEY

1. What are some memories that you have about money from your childhood? Write down two of them (these can be brief.) Look at your life now. Do your memories still impact you now?

2. Make a list of the things you think you can't afford. Pick the first one, and write down three Step Smalls that will take you toward that thing.

3. What are four things you could build if you made more money? (This doesn't have to be physical—you can build a savings account, a new product for your business, etc.)

4. What is your ideal income? What are two Step Smalls that could get you closer to that?

CHAPTER 13–THE UGLY CRY

1. What are some roadblocks you've faced recently? Write them down. Write down how it felt to face them, and how you got through.

2. Write a list of how you can recover from the ugly cry. A funny movie, a day off, a box of chocolates, a long walk, a journal session, music, etc.

3. Give yourself permission to feel all the feels. They are real.

Remind yourself of all the ways life has gotten in the way, and you recovered.

4. List ways that have worked for you to recover from a bad experience. Remember that recovery isn't quick, and that's ok.

Chapter 14—Enjoy the Journey

1. If you struggle to stay in the moment and enjoy the journey, set a calendar reminder to write down ONE thing per day that you enjoyed.
2. Keep a thankful jar. Put slips of paper next to a jar and each day write something down and stick it in the jar.
3. Arrival is a myth as there is always another step. Make a vision board, a list, or keep a journal of all your past accomplishments, current projects, and future dreams. These can be really fun to do. Check out Pinterest for inspiration.
4. 15-Minute Hustle your way to joy every day. Do ANYTHING for 15 minutes daily that brings a smile to your face

Acknowledgments

This book is a small snapshot of my life and business. My ability to do what I love would not be possible without the help of many, many people. I'd like to take this time to thank the ones who directly and indirectly influenced me and helped this book reach your hands.

First, God. Without God, I am nothing. I am grateful for the gifts and abilities I have been given. My prayer is to use them for the greater good of humanity while ultimately leading them back to the source of all good things.

Ben. For being my safe place. For your willingness to jump into the unknown with me. For your grace during all of the late nights and bedside laptop pounding. For being my parachute. For allowing me to fly. For being my forever. You made me a millionaire a long time ago.

LB, Bird, and Sue-boo. Thanks for putting up with many, many "one more minute" pauses. Thank you for giving me a reason to demonstrate what it looks like to push through and do your best. You are my world.

Mom. My biggest fan even at my worst. You always see the good in everything and everyone. I've watched you model resilience, perseverance, and faith over and over with more positivity than any human I know. I couldn't have asked for a better business partner or mom. I want to be you when I grow up.

Amy. For taking the small step of making that first phone call. For pushing me when I couldn't write one more word. For the grace to put up with my crazy quickstart ideas, for being my BFF, for wiping my tears after the ugly cry. For kindly walking me through tech. For being there when I need to outwardly process. For your patience and loyalty. For accountability and turning bright ideas into tangible good. Your impact on my life cannot be measured.

My Fab 4. Keri, Meg, Megan, Cheryl. For giving me a place to be ME without judgment or pretenses. For giving me a space to feel loved, connected and accepted and truly known. For being true, real friends. For all the FUN we've had and will have.

Katie Cross, my writing coach. This would not exist without your accountability, encouragement, and expertise. For pushing me through the hard parts and making me feel normal. Thank you for helping me bring one of my big dreams into reality.

Maureen. Our magical unicorn. You are such a blessing in our lives. Thank you for all the unseen things you do to make our business and life a greater place to be. You are a beautiful woman inside and out.

Rob Watson. For giving me the courage and assistance to take that first *small step*. For teaching me the basics of marketing. For seeing my potential and believing in me when I had absolutely no clue what I was doing. For co-hosting a show with a no-name curly-haired ninja from nowhere. I'm forever grateful.

Chris Green. For taking that first phone call. For writing *Retail Arbitrage* and telling me to write my own book.

Dad. For shaping me into the person I am today and for always letting me know how proud you were of me. I always made it my goal to make you proud.

Jimmy Fallon. Because no one says, "Thank You," quite like you.

Cordelia Blake. For giving me a chance on your show to share my knowledge with the world.

The team. Nathan and Bridgette, Steven, Kelsey, Bernadette. Doing what you do gives me the freedom and joy to do what I love. The ship sinks without you. Much love and appreciation for all you do.

About the Author

Kristin Ostrander is a serial entrepreneur, podcaster, and speaker. She co-founded MommyIncome.com and hosts a weekly podcast titled The Amazon Files. Her grit, hard work, and business savvy have changed her life in ways she never thought possible.

From the emotional low of foreclosing on her first home to scaling new heights with multiple successful businesses, she is determined to make an impact in the lives of others by sharing what she learned along the way.

When she's not taking action in her businesses or supporting others, she can be found spending time with her family along one of the many lakes in Michigan.

Made in the USA
Monee, IL
18 November 2021